HISTORIC TELLURIDE IN RARE PHOTOGRAPHS

Front cover photography: A group of pack burros loaded with wooden crates on Colorado Avenue (see page 74). (W. J. Carpenter photo: Denver Public Library, Western History Department)

Back cover photograph: A group of traveling variety-theatre performers raise a toast for the photographer (see page 151). (Denver Public Library, Western History Department)

Cover design, book design, typography and maps: Laurie Goralka Design

HISTORIC

TELLURIDE
IN
RARE PHOTOGRAPHS

❊ CHRISTIAN J. BUYS ❊

WESTERN
REFLECTIONS, INC.

**H
I
S
T
O
R
I
C

T
E
L
L
U
R
I
D
E

I
N

R
A
R
E

P
H
O
T
O
G
R
A
P
H
S**

Library of Congress Cataloging — Publication Data

Buys, Christian J.
    Historic Telluride in Rare Photographs / by Christian J. Buys. — 2nd ed.
    p. cm.
    ISBN : 1-890437-02-6

    1. Telluride (Colo.) — History — Pictorial works.
  I. Title.

    F784.T44B89 1998   978.8'23
                                    QB198-1079

Library of Congress Catalogue Card Number: 98-87115

Western Reflections, Inc.
P.O. Box 710 • Ouray, CO 81427

Second Edition, 1999

DEDICATION

To my mother, Mina Becker Buys,
my father, Ekdal John Buys,
and my mother-in-law,
Sally VanKuiken

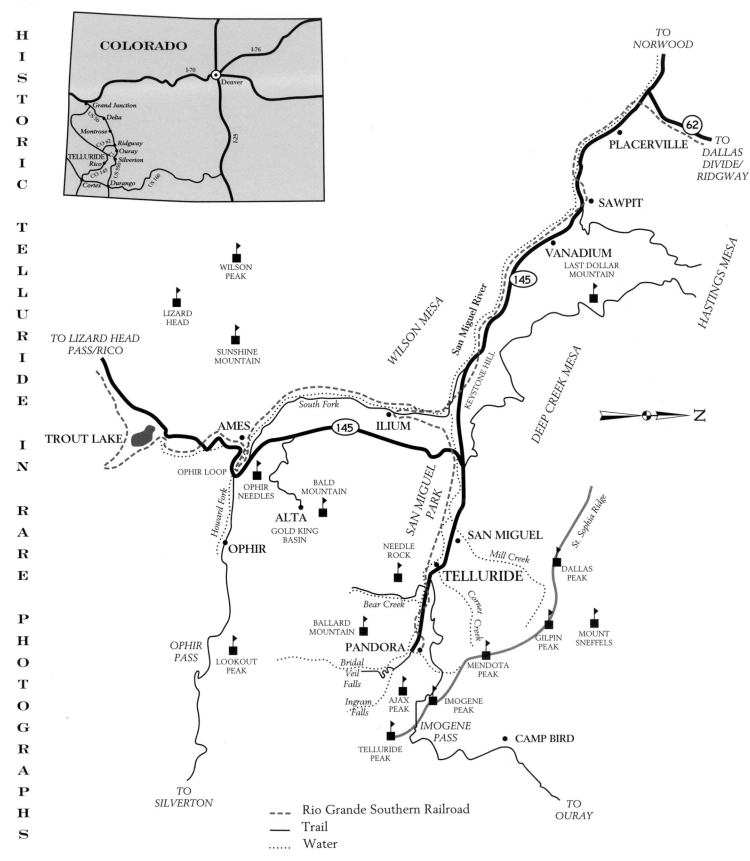

TELLURIDE REGIONAL MAP

COLORADO

TO NORWOOD

TO DALLAS DIVIDE/ RIDGWAY

PLACERVILLE

SAWPIT

VANADIUM

LAST DOLLAR MOUNTAIN

HASTINGS MESA

WILSON PEAK

WILSON MESA

San Miguel River

KEYSTONE HILL

DEEP CREEK MESA

LIZARD HEAD

TO LIZARD HEAD PASS/RICO

SUNSHINE MOUNTAIN

South Fork

AMES

ILIUM

TROUT LAKE

OPHIR LOOP

OPHIR NEEDLES

Howard Fork

BALD MOUNTAIN

SAN MIGUEL PARK

St. Sophia Ridge

ALTA

GOLD KING BASIN

SAN MIGUEL

Mill Creek

DALLAS PEAK

OPHIR

NEEDLE ROCK

TELLURIDE

Cornet Creek

BALLARD MOUNTAIN

Bear Creek

MOUNT SNEFFELS

GILPIN PEAK

PANDORA

MENDOTA PEAK

OPHIR PASS

LOOKOUT PEAK

Bridal Veil Falls

Ingram Falls

AJAX PEAK

IMOGENE PEAK

IMOGENE PASS

CAMP BIRD

TELLURIDE PEAK

TO SILVERTON

TO OURAY

– – – Rio Grande Southern Railroad
—— Trail
...... Water

UPPER SAN MIGUEL MINING DISTRICT

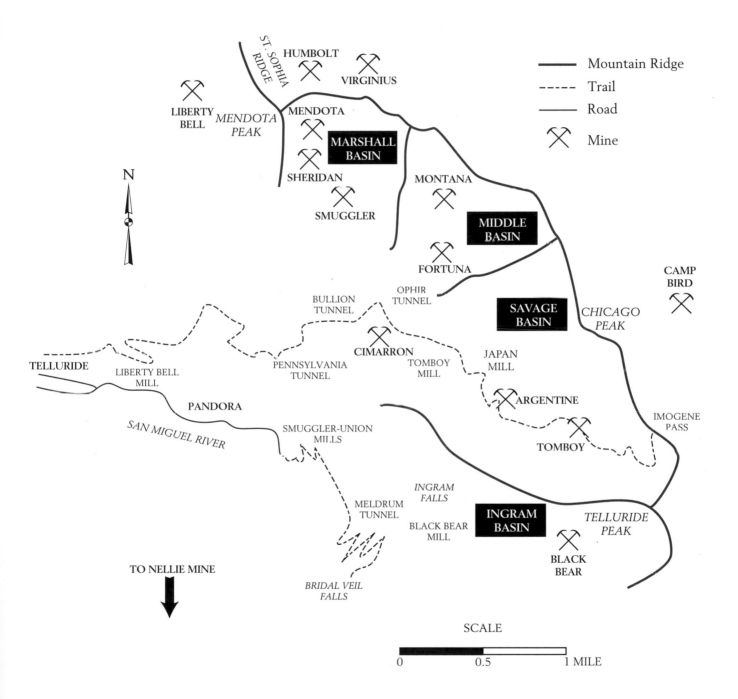

TELLURIDE

1. American House*
2. Anderson, Baisch, and Company Druggists*
3. Original Bank of Telluride
4. Belmont Hotel*
5. Brunswick Saloon*
6. Byers Photography Studio
7. Colorado House*
8. Cosmopolitan Saloon*
9. Cribs
10. Davis House
11. F. D. Work and Company Hardware*
   (*formerly* Stubbs and Jakway)
12. First Congregational Church*
13. First National Bank
14. Golden Rule Store
   (*formerly* National Club Bar)
15. Lone Tree Cemetery
16. Miner's Union Hospital
17. New Sheridan Hotel
18. Nunn House
19. Pick and Gad
20. Quine and Company Druggists
21. Red Men's Hall*
22. Rio Grande Southern Depot
23. Roma Bar
24. San Miguel Courthouse
25. *San Miguel Examiner**
26. San Miguel County Bank*
27. Senate Building
28. Original Sheridan Hotel*
29. Sheridan Opera House
30. Silver Bell
31. St. Patrick's Catholic Church
32. Swede-Finn Hall
33. Telluride Beer Hall*
34. Telluride Historical Museum
   (*formerly* Telluride Community Hospital)
35. Telluride Public School
36. Telluride Town Hall and Fire Station
37. W. B. Van Atta Outfitting
38. Western Colorado Power Company
39. Wunderlich and Dalle Company Bottling
   Works and Beer Storage*
40. Wunderlich House*

* Original structure no longer exists

ACKNOWLEDGEMENTS

P. David and Jan Smith provided me with support and encouragement while I worked on this book. They also supplied me with many historical images and documents from their private collection. Thank you P. David and Jan, it has been — as always — a pleasure. My wife, Beth VanKuiken Buys, and Rita Eisenheim contributed excellent editorial suggestions. I am sincerely grateful to Laurie Goralka for her professional and efficient art direction, design and production. She also made several helpful suggestions and corrections that improved the quality of the original manuscript. Many thanks to Irene R. Visintin, Elvira F. Visintin Wunderlich, Bill Mahoney, and Jerry O'Rourke who graciously took the time to review and to improve various chapters. Dr. James Parker, Martin A. Wenger, John Grimsby, and Dorothy H. Evans also reviewed portions of the manuscript. And I am happy to recognize the late Arlene Reid, who in the mid-1980s shared so much of her time and knowledge of Telluride history with me.

Many individuals generously shared photographs of their personal Telluride legacies, taught me about Telluride history, and allowed me to photograph memorabilia in their private collections. A sincere thanks to Bill Mahoney, Irene R. Visintin, Elvira F. Visintin Wunderlich, Bill Ellicott, Ogda Matson Walter (and Diana Faulker), Joann and the late Wes Leech, Jerry O'Rourke, Dorothy H. Evans, John Grimsby, Alta Cassietto, Dr. James Parker, Eileen Brown, Martin A. Wenger, M. Scott Strain, Ralph Kemper, Robert Sowada, Dan MacKendrick, David Kuhlemeier, Rodger Polley, Nila Horner, and Amore Arcieri.

I am also grateful to several people who helped me assemble and copy images from various photographic archives: Catherine Conrad and Todd Ellison (Center of Southwest Studies, Fort Lewis College, Durango, Colorado); Lori Olson, Daniel Davis, and Carol Bowers (American Heritage Center, University of Wyoming); Kathe Swan and Bruce Hanson (Denver Public Library, Western History Department); Barbara Foley and Rebecca Lentz (Colorado Historical Society, Stephen Hart Library, Denver, Colorado); Judy Prosser-Armstrong and Bess Beran (Museum of Western Colorado, Grand Junction, Colorado); Barb Muntyan (former director of the Ouray County Museum); and the volunteers of the Telluride Historical Museum.

Special thanks to Bill Ellicott, Bill Mahoney, and Jerry O'Rourke for sharing their knowledge of the mining, ranching, and railroading industries in the San Juan region. And to my daughter, Amy E. Buys, who took several high-quality photographs. Bill Huber helped identify the antique gaming machines.

CHAPTER ONE
THE EARLY YE
(1860S-1880S

Utes are swept aside l
seekers flocking into
mineral-rich San Juan Mount

CHAPTER THREE
TURBULENCE I
PARADISE (1900

Deadly labor strikes and
snowslides shatter the
of the mountain town's idyllic
surroundings..............................

PREFACE

TELLURIDE rests in San Miguel Park, one of the most picturesque alpine parks in the West. Nearly six miles long and half a mile wide, the park is traversed by the San Miguel River. In spring the river's muddy-brown water churns through an emerging abundance of brightly colored wild flowers. By summer its hearty turquoise swells splash over smooth boulders, complementing the greenish hues of conifers and salt cedars that intermittently crowd its banks. Come fall the San Miguel's sky-blue water courses more slowly through a cornucopia of oranges, reds, and yellows created by patches of high-altitude aspen and scrub oak. Skittish mule deer lower their heads to drink its bracing liquid while trout flash by. During winter the icy blue river slows, meandering among cornices of windblown snow that blankets the entire six-mile-long flat.

If this splendid kaleidoscope of alpine seasons is not enough to savor, all one has to do is stand anywhere in the small town of Telluride and simply look up. What greets the eye is so magnificent, so inspiring that it confirms the faithfuls' belief in a beneficent god, heightens agnostics' sense of wonder, and causes atheists to marvel. For there above them — closely hugging San Miguel Park — loom massive mountains whose lofty white peaks caress the brilliant azure skies. Already light-headed from the high altitude, visibly awed tourists often stop and stare, blocking the sidewalks in downtown Telluride. Who can blame them? Mainly they gaze east, where bulging creeks rush out of high basins, plummet hundreds of feet, then vanish into a slender silver mist. Close by, enigmatic dark lines zigzag up the impossibly precipitous mountains. Ascending one way, then another into the gray heights, these thread-like traces become fainter, ultimately disappearing into huge basins surrounded by snow-whitened peaks. It takes time, sometimes days, for the mind to appreciate fully this awe-inspiring scene. After all, Telluride's towering mountain backdrop combined with its pristine alpine park setting has few rivals on earth for sheer natural beauty.

While such a dramatic setting provides majestic images for this book, the zigzag lines hold the key to its focus. They are not geologic faults. Rather, those distinct lines are switchbacks in hair-raising trails dynamited and hammered out over a century ago — each inch providing a precipitous path to a fortune, or so the builders hoped. Telluride, in fact, came into existence because of the mineral-rich ores entombed for eons in the massive stone mountains that nearly surround it. That Native Americans first inhabited the park, enjoying its rich bounty for centuries, hardly seemed to matter when word of the new strike spread throughout the United States in the 1870s. There was no stopping the mineral hungry hoards. It was neither the first time, nor would it be the last, that avarice spiced with adventure resulted in the unlawful and unethical displacement of one people by another.

Telluride's fascinating birth and history have been documented in several books and pamphlets. David Lavender's *One Man's West* and *A Rocky Mountain Fantasy, Telluride, Colorado,* Richard and Suzanne Fetter's *Telluride: "From Pick to Powder,"* and Russ Collman's and Dell McKoy's *The R.G.S. [Rio Grande Southern] Story: Volume II — "Telluride, Pandora and* the Mines Above" are four of the best. Harriet Fish Backus's *Tomboy Bride* and Martin G. Wenger's *Recollections of Telluride Colorado* are two of my favorite personalized accounts of the Telluride mining region. Other books, such as *Stampede to Timberline* by Muriel Wolle, *Bostonians and Bullion: The Journal of Robert Livermore, 1892 - 1915* edited by Gene Gressely, *"I Hauled These Mountains in Here!"* by Frances and Dorothy Wood, *Mountain Mysteries: The Ouray Odyssey* by Marvin Gregory and P. David Smith, and *The Rio Grande Southern Railroad* by Josie Crum contain intriguing and informative sections on Telluride history. Most of these publications (especially the ambitious, multi-volume *The R.G.S. Story*) contain historic images of Telluride. For years, however, I had hoped for a general pictorial history of Telluride and vicinity. Given its unequalled setting and rich history, what mountain mining town deserves it more? Finally, I decided to undertake the task.

A rich, rewarding experience awaited me. What more can one ask — of those of us who are fascinated by historic images — than to sort through hundreds of old photographs of the Telluride region. My quest for historic images first took me to the photographic archives at the Center of Southwest Studies at Fort Lewis College in Durango, Colorado, then to the American Heritage Center at the University of Wyoming in Laramie. After visits to the photographic archives in the Colorado Historical Society and the Denver Public Library, I made several pleasant journeys to the Telluride Historical Museum, a repository for a bonanza of photographs. The Museum of Western Colorado in Grand Junction, Colorado, the Walker

Photographic Collection at Main Street Photography in Montrose, Colorado, and the Ouray County Museum in Ouray, Colorado, also held some classic images that I have included in this book. So too, I had the good fortune to have several generous individuals, who are equally fascinated by Telluride's past, allow me to include their personal family photographs and memorabilia. Of course the photographs herein are only a small fraction of the photographs I uncovered. The more excellent photographs I found, the more frustrated I became by having to choose among them.

Finally, during the past three decades I have had the privilege of hiking in the high country above Telluride with my son (Matthew), my daughter (Amy), my dog (Sherlock), and a few good friends (Bill Ellicott, Cliff Britton, Walt Kelley, Scott Strain, and Ben Kirsten). We have huffed and puffed into every remote basin we could reach. Our greatest rewards have been visual. On a clear day nothing compares to sitting down on a stony ridge, with marmots' scolding barks echoing in a high cirque, to gaze down upon waterfalls, basins, and forests with tiny Telluride and San Miguel Park stretching west. Nor does anything spur the visual imagination like the discovery of a long-forgotten miner's cabin, a hidden tram tower, or an abandoned glory hole. One's mind fills with images of what it used to be like in the heyday of mining, not only in Telluride, but up on these secluded, nearly inaccessible benches and slopes. As you turn the pages of this book, I hope that you, too, will experience some of these same emotions — the delight of visual treasures, the exhilaration of discovery.

CHAPTER ONE

THE EARLY YEARS

In the early 1860s the Utes must have watched, wondering, as the Charles Baker party snaked its way over present-day Ophir Pass into their treasured alpine park. They had not seen strangers like these in their homeland since the few fur-traders whom they had forced out decades earlier. Baker's party didn't stay long in the valley (if, in fact, they reached San Miguel Park), so the Utes could not have known that this disheveled band of Anglo-American prospectors was a harbinger of a massive wave of humanity that would soon inundate their homeland and drive them away.

The Utes' demise happened fast and unfairly. By 1868 they had signed a treaty with the United States that "granted" them about one-quarter of present-day Western Colorado, including the — unbeknownst at the time — mineral-rich San Juan Mountains. By 1873, however, "the mining interest became so strong" that they reluctantly ceded four million acres of the San Juan Mountains to the United States for a perpetual yearly annuity of $25,000, mostly in the form of goods. Finally, during the late summer in 1881, the few Utes remaining in present-day western Colorado embarked on a forced exodus to Utah Territory. Most of them could not bear to look back at their beloved valleys and mountains, now swarming with mineral-hungry intruders.

Earlier, in 1872, Linnard Remine and a few companions — possibly the first men to enter the San Miguel Valley since the fur traders — illegally had started placer mining on the Ute Reservation. Thoughts of the resulting devastation to the Utes' way of life did not enter their minds. Rather, they carefully cultivated a friendship with the powerful Utes who came each summer and fall to hunt and fish in game-rich San Miguel Park. Years later Remine said the Utes told him of early Spanish mining activity in the park. Coupled with the unconfirmed rumors of the "discovery of old Spanish tools on a certain vein opening" in the nearby mountains, Remine's report has fueled rumors of hidden Spanish treasure and lost mines ever since.

It is no rumor that the government-sponsored Hayden Survey group mapped the San Miguel Valley in 1874, or that in 1875 John Fallon somehow scaled a spectacular 13,000 foot high craggy granite barrier near St. Sophia Ridge. Then Fallon managed to make it down into Marshall Basin from the east. He wasn't interested in panning for a few nuggets. He sought the mother lode. Fallon staked out five claims in Marshall Basin in October 1875. Mining-town myth holds that his first shipment of ore to Silverton, where he officially filed his claims, put $10,000 into his pockets. The precise value of that

(1860s-1880s)

original ore carried by Fallon's small string of burros doesn't really matter. What matters is that Fallon had found a rich deposit of gold ore. The rush was on.

By the summer of 1875 over three hundred men were feverishly working the gravel along the San Miguel River, while many others scoured the mountains nearby. Great lodes, like the Sheridan, Smuggler-Union, Liberty Bell, Tomboy, and Gold King, were soon claimed. As the miners burrowed the tunnels and shafts deeper into the mountains, hydraulic mining — blasting the earth with powerful streams of water — methodically carved up the banks of the San Miguel River below. By 1877, with railroad tourist guides touting the easy riches in the San Juan Mountains, carloads of starry-eyed fortune seekers arrived in Pueblo, Colorado. There they transferred to "emigrant trains," meaning stages, coaches, freight wagons, and anything else with wheels, to get them to the booming San Juan region. Many arrived in the nascent San Miguel, soon to be called San Miguel City. About a year later and about a mile east another small mining settlement sprang up. First called Columbia, this town's schizophrenic journey to claim its permanent name, Telluride, did not officially end until 1887.

During the 1880s the Telluride mining region grew steadily. What little flat ground could be found at lower elevations quickly blossomed into small multi-cultural, mining-support communities. Taking names like Ames, Rico, Ophir, Sawpit, and Placerville, their muddy streets teemed with freight wagons and strings of heavily loaded pack animals bound for high-country mines. Far above, resembling lines of ants, still more strings of pack animals laden with high-grade ore made their way down switchbacks that clung precariously to the precipitous mountains. One misstep meant a journey into oblivion.

Mining, bawdiness, and booze dominated the tenor of Telluride in the early 1880s. Soon, in accord with the natural evolution of mining towns, a more domesticated element made its presence known. Hotels, banks, law firms, schools, police departments, fire departments, theatres, telegraph lines, and even a few small churches took their place alongside the saloons and gaming halls. The civilizing element, however, did not prevent the criminal Butch Cassidy and his gang from robbing the San Miguel County Bank in 1889. Nor did it stifle the rows of "cribs" along East Pacific Avenue that catered to the hoards of men eager for a drink and feminine company after grueling weeks of dangerous and hard labor in the mines above.

Sacred mountains

In the early 1880s few people expressed remorse over the Utes' forced removal from the San Juan Mountain region. In late August, 1881, a local newspaper extolled: "Sunday morning the Utes bid adieu to their old hunting grounds and folded their tents, rounded up their dogs, sheep, goats, ponies and traps, and took up the line of march for their new reservation, followed by General MacKenzie and his troops. This is an event that has long and devoutly been prayed for by our people" *(Ouray Times)*. A jubilant Otto Mears, noted local toll-road and railroad builder, rode with the military escort.

General John Pope, who witnessed the Utes' removal from their homelands, did not celebrate. Years later he lamented: "The whites who had collected, in view of their [Utes] removal, were so eager and so unrestrained by common decency that it was absolutely necessary to use military force to keep them off the reservation until the Indians were fairly gone." Two decades earlier the Utes had signed a treaty with the Colorado territorial governor which promised them portions of their sacred San Juan Mountains and the Uncompahgre drainage region forever. (Colorado Historical Society, Stephen Hart Library.)

Rotten goods

After the United States government wrested the Utes from the San Juan Mountain region, it "granted" them reservations in southern Colorado and Utah Territory for perpetuity. Indian supply trains, like the one shown here on an early stereocard, were to bring the Utes a "perpetual yearly annuity" of $25,000 — mostly in the form of goods. The supply trains seldom came. When the trains did arrive, according to Territorial Governor Cunningham, the goods proved to be "disgracefully worthless, rotten, and disgusting, and might reasonably have been made the ground of revocation of the treaty." (Thurlow photo: Courtesy of Joann and Wes Leech)

Cantonment on Uncompahgre, Colorado.   Nov 8, 1886   (Fort Crawford)   No. 10

Fort Crawford: A symbol of transition

Soldiers built Fort Crawford (first called the Cantonment on the Uncompahgre) on the Ute Reservation along the Uncompahgre River south of present-day Montrose, Colorado. It housed the troops who escorted the remaining Utes from the San Juan Mountain region in 1881. Although sacrosanct to the Utes, for years hundreds of miners had already been feverishly blasting and digging their way into the nearby foothills and mountains. After the Utes were removed, there was no reason for the stronghold. Soldiers finally dismantled Fort Crawford in 1890. (Denver Public Library, Western History Department).

Soldiers' quarters

Men of Company G, 10th Infantry, lounge in front of their quarters at Fort Crawford. After the removal of the Utes, commanders at the fort created projects to keep the restless troops occupied. (Denver Public Library, Western History Department) (A.E. Buys photos: Author's collection)

Chief Ouray and his wife, Chipeta

Intelligent, dignified, and gracious, Chief Ouray and Chipeta held off the white man's onslaught as long as they could. It was said of the sophisticated and multilingual Ouray: "Never in all his dealings with the whites did he show himself other than their friend." Indeed, some say he saved the Utes from complete annihilation. After he died in 1880 the demise of the once great Ute nation followed quickly. Today the Utes occupy reservations in southern Colorado and northeastern Utah. (Courtesy of P. David Smith)

CHAPTER ONE: THE EARLY YEARS (1860s-1880s)

More than a man and his burro

Alone prospector and his reluctant burro seem harmless enough, gamely trudging up an incline. Yet this image represents the essence of the urge that nearly destroyed the Ute nation and decimated the pristine San Juan environment. Wherever a lucky prospector turned his dreams of mineral wealth into reality, fortune seekers from all over the United States, and often Europe, soon inundated the region. The San Juan "strike" of the mid-1870s held true to this pattern. (J. Byers photo: Courtesy of Walker Collection)

He thought he had killed a man

Linnard Remine was one of the first men to enter San Miguel Park in search of gold. Long-time Telluride resident Martin G. Wenger, who as a young boy knew Remine, recounts that Remine journeyed into the remote Telluride region "as a result of a fight incident in the mining camp of Creede. Someone had jumped his mining claim there and in the following fight Remine thought he had killed the man. He left Creede and worked his way to [the] present town of Delta. After finding out from a source some time later [that] he had not killed the man, he moved to the San Juans hoping to find ore there, thus his entry into the San Miguel Valley."

From Delta Remine led a small band of his friends over the longer and lower present-day Dallas Divide around Last Dollar Mountain. Then he hiked along the San Miguel River into San Miguel Park. There, in the early 1870s, he and his companions cut "enough grass to feed their trail-weary packstock" (Lavender, 1987). Remine told Wenger that they "started placer mining and they each made about $15.00 a day panning for gold" (Wenger, 1978). Remine's appearance and surroundings in this 1920s photograph shows that Remine eventually became a "strange acting" hermit. (Telluride Historical Museum)

Remine's cabin

With this primitive cabin as his base, Linnard Remine staked several claims and ran trap lines. "Remine said that when he first visited the San Miguel Valley it was located on the Ute Indian Reservation [although this did not deter him from illegally building a cabin]. Each summer and fall the Utes came to hunt game which abounded in the valley. Deer, wild turkeys and grouse were plentiful and the river abounded in fish" (Wenger, 1978).

One wonders what would have happened in the San Miguel Valley if the Utes had organized themselves politically and confronted the invaders with high-quality lawyers of their own kind. (Telluride Historical Museum)

Hayden's Survey

In 1874 Hayden's Survey party put the San Juan Valley on a detailed map. The maps that resulted from this survey were probably used to stake the first placer claim in the San Miguel Mining District on August 23, 1875. (Reprinted from *Harper's Weekly*, October 12, 1878: Author's collection)

CHAPTER ONE: THE EARLY YEARS (1860s-1880s)

Come one, come all

By the summer of 1875 Remine and his companions were no longer alone. Over 300 men had invaded the pristine San Miguel Valley to work the gravel along the San Miguel River, while many others feverishly scoured the mountains. This same year John Fallon somehow scaled a spectacular 13,000 foot high craggy granite barrier southeast of St. Sophia Ridge, then hiked down into Marshall Basin from the east. Fallon wasn't interested in panning for a few nuggets. He sought the mother lode. Fallon staked five claims in Marshall Basin: Emerald, Tripple, Sheridan, Ansborough, and Fallon. The Sheridan became the shining star. Mining-town myth holds that his first pack train of ore to Silverton, where he filed his claims, put $10,000 into his pockets. The precise value of the ore carried by Fallon's small string of donkeys doesn't really matter. What matters is that Fallon had found a rich deposit of gold ore.

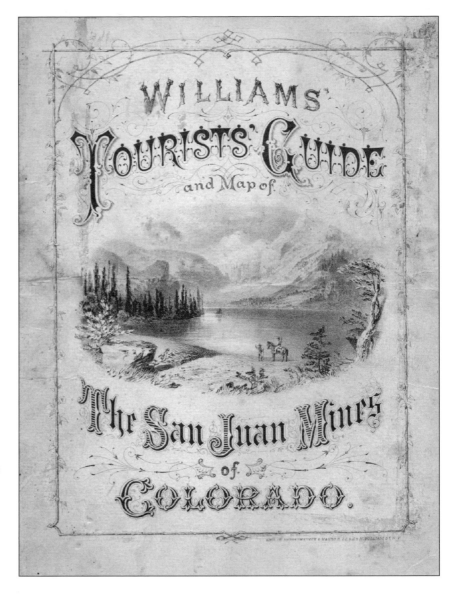

The following year, below Fallon's claims in Marshall Basin, the Pandora Mine (eventually a small mill town) was staked out by James Carpenter and Thomas Lowthian on the eastern edge of San Miguel Park. Also in 1876, according to Colorado historian Robert Brown, "one J. B. Ingram was prospecting in the [Marshall] [B]asin. It occurred to him at the time that the Union and Sheridan claims exceeded their legal allowance. Taking his own measurements, he discovered that both had about five hundred feet of land that was not legally theirs. Putting down his own stake upon the surplus ground, he named his property [boldly] the Smuggler. This incredible bit of good fortune resulted in one of the region's richest mines." Then W. L. Cornett discovered the promising Liberty Bell gold mine high at the head of Cornet Creek (named after him, but spelled with one less "t"). News of these phenomenal discoveries in the San Juans spread fast. By 1877, the rush was really on.

"Williams' Tourists' Guide" (shown here) quickly got in on the act. "Until September, 1872," the guide's author wrote, "the entire section known as 'the San Juan Country' was part of the Ute Indian reservation. At that time the Indian title was extinguished, and the country thrown open to settlement." The fifty-page guide describes the "San Juan Country" in detail. The reliability of such guides suffered because they were often penned by persons who had never been to the destinations they described. (Author's collection)

Railroad propaganda

In 1877 several railroads advertised passage to the San Juan mining region in Williams' popular tourist guides. Each railroad company promised comfortable and punctual connections to Denver or Pueblo where fortune seekers could board the Denver & Rio Grande Railway (D&RGRy) to its "Western Terminus [end of the tracks], where all the San Juan Freighting and Outfitting is done." The D&RGRy's ad (above) promised "No delays on the Route" to "The Best and Richest Mining District in the World."

Gold-hungry enthusiasts eager to believe such propaganda undoubtedly trusted the guidebook's weather reports as well: "The climate of the San Juan is one of the finest in the world. The pure, bracing mountain air expands the lungs, gives vivacity, energy, and robust health. Malaria is unknown. The temperature is moderate. The winters are not more severe than in other portions of the State, and even thus far the winters of 1875-6-7 have been milder in the San Juan country than elsewhere of same altitude in Colorado." (Author's collection)

CHAPTER ONE: THE EARLY YEARS (1860s-1880s)

Idyllic scenes

Idyllic mining scenes, like this combined with the railroads' propaganda, provided the impetus for thousands of people to head for the San Juans. Here a cozy-looking stagecoach travels past numerous miners panning their fortunes in a crisp, clean mountain environment. One of the miners waves a friendly hat at the passengers, as though beckoning them to join him. Water pours from a long sluice — undoubtedly sparkling with gold. In the background surrealistic cliffs reach out to touch each other across a narrow canyon. (Reprinted from *Grip-Sack Guide of Colorado (1880)*: Author's collection).

CHAPTER ONE: THE EARLY YEARS (1860s-1880s)

Impossible to exaggerate

The early guidebooks could not exaggerate the beauty of the San Juans. Drawings in an early *Harper's Weekly* show some of the high country near present-day Telluride described by the *Williams' Tourist's Guide* as "a scene of beauty the imagination cannot depict." (*Harper's Weekly*, June 11, 1887: Courtesy of P. David Smith)

CHAPTER ONE: THE EARLY YEARS (1860s-1880s)

Blasting the gold-bearing gravel

Once the miners had panned out the surface gold in the San Miguel River near present-day Telluride, destructive hydraulic mining (washing the ore-bearing gravel out of the hillsides) started in earnest in 1877. Keystone Hill, at the top of the cascades (about three miles west of present-day Telluride), had the most active hydraulic mining after "the Wheeler and Kimball Ditch was completed to carry water to the claims" (Brown, 1968).

Hydraulic mining techniques required tremendous water pressure. By diverting water from mountain streams or lakes into wooden flumes high above the claims, then funneling it into narrower pipes, the water burst full-force out of the nine-inch-diameter nozzles used on most claims. No motors were employed. (Reprinted from *Telluride and San Miguel County*, 1894: Courtesy of P. David Smith)

CHAPTER ONE: THE EARLY YEARS (1860S-1880S)

Impounding dams

The photographer scribbled "Impounded Dams on Gold Run Placer" across the bottom of this photograph. Stretching across the San Miguel River, dams like these provided another source of water under pressure for hydraulic mining downstream. Located east of Telluride, the Gold Run Placer claim is shown on a San Miguel County Mining Claims map from the 1920s. (Author's photo: Courtesy of Bill Mahoney) (Denver Public Library, Western History Department)

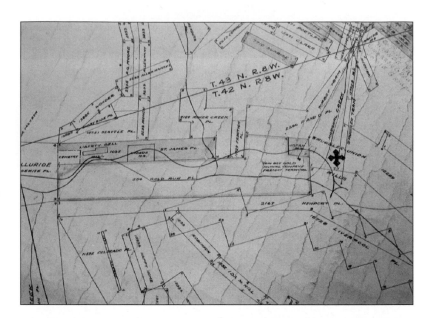

Lumber for houses

Sam Blair ran one of the region's earliest sawmills on Mill Creek. The sawmill's front gable structure had horizontally sawn, unhewn log siding. It provided wood for several of the homes in San Miguel, the first settlement in the valley. Many of the homes and businesses in Columbia (two miles east of San Miguel) were also constructed with wood from this classic old mill. Columbia (present-day Telluride) was incorporated by the unanimous decision of all twenty-eight voters on July 18, 1878. (Telluride Historical Museum)

CHAPTER ONE: THE EARLY YEARS (1860s-1880s)

Then there was "Telluride"

By the mid-1880s Columbia consisted mainly of wood frame structures, with the exception of the newly built brick courthouse on Colorado Avenue, Columbia's atypically wide main street. With the aid of a magnifying glass, one can spot the American House Hotel, the large rectangular building that faces north on Colorado Avenue.

Even today sources differ in their accounts of this early mining community's schizophrenic journey to be named Telluride. Most accounts agree that San Miguel, soon to be San Miguel City, was first settled about two miles west of Columbia during 1875 and 1876. In 1878 Columbia sprang up about two miles east of San Miguel City. Located closer to the mines, it would soon supplant San Miguel City (population "5 women and 200 men by 1880") in significance and size. Yet in 1885 the map supplied with Crofutt's popular *Grip-Sack Guide of Colorado (1885)* shows only "San Miguel" (without "City"). Columbia is also shown, but it appears in conjunction with a town called "Folsum."

It turns out that Folsom was originally called Newport, which was located immediately east of Columbia. In time Folsom became Pandora

(named after an early claim), where the great mills were built. Most of the confusion, however, hinged on the location of a proper post office — a major source of pride for any mining-town community. Trouble was, the name "Columbia" was already taken by a California town. Yet the Washington postal authorities refused to change the post office name from Columbia to Telluride, as some of the town's people wished. ("Telluride" was taken from the nonmetallic element tellurium which is virtually nonexistent in the region.) In the early 1880s the post office of Telluride (the name preferred by the majority of locals) was actually transferred to the town of Folsom. So people from Telluride had to go to Folsum to pick up their mail.

"Who straightened out Telluride's identity is unknown, but on December 13, 1880, the post office, Telluride, was returned to its original location, although the town itself still clung to the name Columbia" (Lavender, 1987). Mercifully, on June 4, 1887, Telluride officially became "Telluride," a name — then and now — unique in America. (T. McKee photo: Denver Public Library, Western History Department)

A wide main street

Unlike many early San Juan mining towns, Telluride had a spacious main street, Colorado Avenue (even today temporary parking for deliveries is allowed in the middle of the avenue). Joseph Collier set up his tripod and camera facing east to record this rare image of many of Telluride's (technically Columbia's) earliest businesses. On the south side of Colorado Avenue, Denison's grocery store stands next to S. R. Fitgarralo's law office. Farther down are Tryan's Hardware, Oderfeld's General Merchandise shop, and a meat market. Across Colorado Avenue are the Telluride House, Stewart's Hardware, and the American House (the tallest structure), a familiar point of reference in early panoramas of the mining camp. Telluride's infamous post office, a bakery, and a grocery store stand farther down the block.

Two men and a boy on the boardwalk under Denison's sign stopped to stare intently at the camera, as did several men from across the street. The man at the left-center of the photograph continued to cross the street, causing his image to blur. Several pack burros gathered on Telluride's dirt thoroughfare are most likely waiting to ascend the steep trails to the mines. (J. Collier photo: Denver Public Library, Western History Department)

365. TELLURIDE

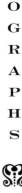

H
I
S
T
O
R
I
C

T
E
L
L
U
R
I
D
E

I
N

R
A
R
E

P
H
O
T
O
G
R
A
P
H
S

Telluride's first family?

This photograph of the Umpskad family in their oxcart carries the notation, "First Family to Telluride." If this is true, some locals probably welcomed them as the first sign of a civilizing influence, others probably preferred Telluride to remain the way it was — with mining, bawdiness, and booze dominating the tenor of the town. (Telluride Historical Museum)

Wagon Train, Telluride, Colo. About 1880

Freighters ruled

Dave Wood's ox teams haul large pipes, most likely destined for high mines, through downtown Telluride. During the 1870s and 1880s freighters such as Dave Wood comprised the life line of Telluride and the mines. Without them, no one would have prospered.

Two of Wood's daughters, Frances and Dorothy, wrote the history of their father's transportation company in a splendid book, *I Hauled These Mountains in Here!* They recount: "Wood played an historic part in opening up the western slope of the Great Divide. His huge freight wagons hauled in food, machinery, dynamite, coal — everything needed at the mines." (Courtesy of P. David Smith)

CHAPTER ONE: THE EARLY YEARS (1860s-1880s)

Dave Wood, Magnolia Route

Wood's canvas-covered wagons carried the names of the places they served. "Telluride" appears on the second wagon in this unusual tandem. The flat terrain and low hills in the background indicate the photograph was taken near Montrose. (Courtesy of P. David Smith)

Head Office, Montrose

Dave Wood, standing beside the buggy, operated his many-tentacled freight business from Montrose, Colorado. The huge livery barn (left) and corrals in Montrose accommodated over 100 head of stock. Included in this count were twenty-mule teams, all matched. Wood's "Transportation Lines" prospered and brought prosperity to the area. Records indicate that the company grossed over $150,000 during three months in 1882.

"He freighted over roads that were scarcely more than trails, and where there was no road at all he built one. Where there were no towns he helped build those, too, and added his freight stations and warehouses" (Wood and Wood, 1977). In fact, Dave Wood (right) spent $30,000 to have a private freighting road built across Horsefly Mesa to Leonard in order to avoid some of the worst of the rough miles between Montrose and Telluride as well as severe problems caused by floods. No one is certain why he named it "The Magnolia Route." (Courtesy of Walker Collection) (Courtesy of P. David Smith)

"Rocky Mountain canaries"

This time-worn photograph features another gathering of Dave Wood's freight wagons in Telluride, although other freighters thrived in the booming mining town as well. "The principal operator in this 'packing business,' as it was called, was a prosperous, popular and straight shooting (both ways) bachelor named Ed Lavender. He was a cattleman and a good hunter. In later years he became the step-father of the well-known author of Western history, David Lavender" (Belsey, 1962).

From Telluride, "big Missouri mules, Rocky Mountain canaries (burros) and six-horse-draft teams pulling freight wagons (similar to the Death Valley borax vehicles) packed and hauled machinery, lumber and mine timbers, dynamite, sides of beef and whole hogs, all other food and a myriad of supplies" (Belsey, 1962). (H. Reid photo: Colorado Historical Society, Stephen Hart Library)

Commissioner visits Telluride

With his dapper mustache and tie Louie Wyman, county commissioner from Silverton, Colorado, poses on horseback by a false-front Telluride store. American flags flutter in the wind behind him. The flags suggest that the politician's visit during the 1880s may have been on the Fourth of July, or perhaps a county election day.

In early 1881 Dolores County, which included Telluride and Silverton, splintered away from the unwieldy Ouray County. Two years later the state legislature created another smaller county, San Miguel, in which Telluride remains. (Denver Public Library, Western History Department)

Old toll road

Commissioner Wyman probably rode over this steep, rocky toll road between Silverton to Ophir. Today four-wheel drive vehicles easily negotiate this old toll road, now called Ophir Pass, during late summer and early fall. Like other high passes in the San Juans, deep snow renders it impassible most of the year. (J. Collier photo: Denver Public Library, Western History Collection)

CHAPTER ONE: THE EARLY YEARS (1860s-1880s)

Treacherous going

Before Imogene Pass opened above Camp Bird Mine, those who wanted to take the short route from Ouray to Telluride had to cross over formidable pinnacles southeast of St. Sophia Ridge. "Virginius Mine Showing Pass to Telluride" is written faintly on the right half of this early stereocard. Virginius Basin is on the Ouray side of the St. Sophia Ridge.

"The ridge is also visible from Telluride and the old trail to Telluride crosses its southern end. [An inverted "V" marks the spot on each side of the stereocard.] The trail forks after crossing the ridge, but both branches go to Telluride, the left fork via Marshall Basin and right fork via the Liberty Bell Mine and Cornet Creek. The ridge itself is unsafe to climb because of crumbling rock and even on the trail the climb is rough and extremely dangerous. In the late 1800s, the accepted practice for one way of travel between Ouray and Telluride was to ride a horse to the Virginius, then walk across the ridge to the Smuggler Mine where the traveler got another horse to ride to Telluride" (Gregory and Smith, 1984).

This author and a friend, Walter Kelley, can attest that the old trail from Ouray to Telluride is still unsafe to hike. Our ascent ended less than 100 vertical feet from the top of the ridge, because we could no longer find reasonable footholds in the precipitous talus trail. We dubbed this upper portion, "Chicken Ridge." (Museum of Western Colorado)

Tale of two seasons

"John Donnellan and William Everett were the locators [of the Mendota Mine above the Sheridan] and they, with a third man, worked a lease on the Sheridan during the winter of 1878, and ran 100 feet on what is now the main level of the Sheridan. They took out considerable ore which by careful sorting could pay the high charges of freighting and yet leave a good margin" (*Telluride and San Miguel County*, 1894).

In 1880 John Fallon sold the Sheridan for $50,000 to some people in Milwaukee, Wisconsin. They, in turn, sold the property for $250,000 in 1883 to a syndicate of Englishmen based in Shanghai, China. Shown here in both images are the Mendota Mine workings in the foreground with the Sheridan Mine workings just below. (The Mendota, Sheridan, and Smuggler-Union all tapped into the same extended vein.) Although taken from slightly different views, these photographs high in Marshall Basin tell a tale of two seasons. Winter usually lasted seven to eight months a year. Most years the snow never completely melted. (Photos: Denver Public Library, Western History Department)

CHAPTER ONE: THE EARLY YEARS (1860s-1880s)

A prominent merchant

W.B. Van Atta opened his business on the northwest corner of Colorado Avenue and Pine Street in 1883. He promoted his store as the "Up-to-date Outfitter," offering a "complete line of clothing for men and women, along with a fine assortment of yard goods." Van Atta quickly became one of the more important businessmen in Telluride. Stories circulated that he once sold $2,000 worth of merchandise in a single evening. (Reprinted from *Telluride and San Miguel County*, 1894)

An assortment of goods

An old receipt testifies to the variety of merchandise available in Van Atta's store. Personal and household items on this list include a nightgown, fishnet curtains, hose, underwear, carpet sweeper, and thread. The fine print under "The Outfitter" makes it clear that all credit must be settled each month, or a two percent interest charge per month (or twenty-four percent per year) would be assessed. (Courtesy of P. David Smith)

Interior of Van Atta's home

The Van Atta family spent many enjoyable hours in their cluttered and comfortable home. A stack of scholarly books, journals, and a dictionary indicate an intellectual atmosphere. No surprise, since the 1890 state business directory lists "Miss Elanor Vanatta (sic)" as a Telluride physician. In this room the Van Atta family must also have recounted their harrowing experience along the Magnolia Route. David Wood told the story: "Part of the road to Telluride was covered with deep snow in winter. The stage company was trying to operate its line to Telluride with buckboards and horses. At the snows I transferred my loads (freight) to big sleds. My teams with their sleds caught one of the buckboards stalled one day in deep snow, with no chance to get out. W. B. Van Atta, a prominent merchant of Telluride, and his wife and child were in it, in danger of perishing in the snow. Of course my drivers took care of them and took them in to Netherlys [one of Wood's way stations], where they had comfort, warmth, and food" (quoted in Wood and Wood, 1977). (Telluride Historical Museum)

Pioneer Charles F. Painter

Charles F. Painter served as Telluride's first mayor, first county clerk, and publisher of the first newspaper (*The Journal*). He also oversaw a successful insurance, loan, and abstract company for several decades. In 1889 Painter's ornate stationery heading bespoke of his success. Close inspection of the names on the business receipt from 1909 confirm that it was strictly a family business. Painter's talented grandson, David Lavender, became a prolific Western writer. The Painter family is shown here on "chair rock" near the high school. (Receipts courtesy of P. David Smith) (Photo courtesy of Bill Mahoney)

Fourth of July celebration

Telluride, like most towns in America, seized the opportunity to celebrate the Fourth of July. In 1887, Telluride (above) turned out its brass band, mounted troops, fire-hose cart, and flags galore. It had reason to celebrate.

A popular tourist guide wrote: "Telluride is the commercial centre for the immense wealth of this county, and if we mistake not her citizens realize this fact, and will do all in their power to encourage and attract business. The lode mine ores are galena, grey copper, iron, and zinc, free gold and silver; and it is a camp where work can be done at all seasons. In fact, Telluride has a bright and promising future" (*Grip-Sack Guide of Colorado (1885)*).(American Heritage Center, University of Wyoming)

CHAPTER ONE: THE EARLY YEARS (1860s-1880s)

Fashionable portrait photography

Portrait photographs proved especially popular in mining towns. Here L. D. Emery of Telluride poses before a painted, stone block wall backdrop typical for this period. Real dried grass covers the floor. Emery's 44-40 caliber, 1873 Winchester rifle can be identified by the distinct line on the breech. Since this Winchester model was about forty-two inches long, Emery must have been short. His leather chaps afforded his legs protection from bushes and helped keep them warm in the winter. This style of chaps carried the name "shotgun chaps" because of its stovepipe shape. Obviously, Emery earned his living as a cowboy, not a miner. (Denver Public Library, Western History Department)

CHAPTER ONE: THE EARLY YEARS (1860s-1880s)

Country schoolhouse

Shown here is a one-room schoolhouse in the vicinity of Telluride. Neither its precise location nor the identity of the schoolchildren — and the boy on a burro next to the two men — are known. The board and batten construction with a front gable structure and two sash pane windows on the sides is typical for the period. A stovepipe protrudes from the steeply canted shingle roof.

There is no mention of a school in an early description of Telluride: "Seat of San Miguel county, on the upper San Miguel river, surrounded by high mountains covered with timber and filled with rich minerals; altitude, 8,410 feet. It contains one bank, stores of all kinds, several hotels, one 20 and one 40 stamp mill, one weekly newspaper — the *News*, and a

population of about 1,400, most of whom are engaged in mining" (*Grip-Sack Guide of Colorado (1885)*). Actually the Telluride (then called Columbia) area school district was formed four years earlier (August 10, 1881) in a portion of Ouray County. Lillian Blair served as the first teacher and held classes in W. A. Taylor's house, which was located across from where St. Patrick's Church now stands. In 1883 the people of Telluride built a wooden schoolhouse for $3,000 (clearly not the one shown here), to be "replaced by a brick one [see page 104] which later housed the town hall." Currently mounted on the town hall roof, the old school bell serves as a fire alarm bell. (Denver Public Library, Western History Department)

The first postmaster

Imagine the confusion and controversy that James P. Redick, Telluride's first "postmaster and news-dealer" (left), faced until Columbia finally changed its name to Telluride in 1887. According to Alta Cassietto, Redick's daughter had the distinction of being the first child born in Telluride (although it was still officially named Columbia). Alta Cassietto served as Telluride's postmaster from 1934 to 1970. Her parents gave her the name of the mine where she was born — Alta. (Courtesy of Alta Cassietto)

Early post office

Due to a lack of funds, for several years Telluride postmasters had to sort letters in the back of J. B. Anderson's Drug and Jewelry Store. Two flags hang over the receiving window where long lines of miners waited impatiently to receive word, any word, from home. The importance people in remote mining camps placed on receiving mail regularly is hard to overstate. That is why even in winter mail carriers braved the severest of high-country conditions to do what now has become a cliche', to "get the mail through."

Warnings of severe weather on December 23, 1883, did not prevent the mail carrier from making his regular trek on snowshoes from Silverton to Ophir. He knew how much his packages and Christmas letters would mean to the people in Ophir. It was already storming when he left. "When he did not arrive [in Ophir], searching parties went out, but they could find no trace of him. During the summer as soon as the snow melted the search was resumed, but with no success. Not until August, 1885, did another search party uncover his body at the bottom of a snowbank — the mailsack still strapped to his back" (Wolle, 1949). (Courtesy of Alta Cassietto)

Life was not worth living without her

John B. Frasher (above) served as Telluride's county treasurer and second postmaster. His sorrow over the unexpected death of his beloved wife was too much for him to bear. Frasher walked down to the Lone Tree Cemetery and took his own life on her grave. (Courtesy of Alta Cassietto).

CHAPTER ONE: THE EARLY YEARS (1860s-1880s)

Saloons galore

In 1887 Telluride had ten saloons but no churches. The interior of the
Olson Saloon (possibly The Mint or Senate Saloon) in later years is shown
above. (Telluride Historical Museum)

The bank Butch robbed

In the summer of 1889 Butch Cassidy and his gang relieved the San Miguel County Bank (narrow wood building with "Bank" sign above) of its monthly miners' payroll money — approximately $24,000. (Telluride Historical Museum)

The Wild Bunch

A posse headed by none other than the owner of the bank, Lucien Nunn, took off in hot pursuit of Butch and his Wild Bunch. "The race was close. This was evident a few months later when the carcasses of four horses were found still tied to a tree. They had been left for relay, but the outlaws had been crowded into a different getaway route and were unable to pick them up. The robbers did rest for a bit at Trout Lake but disappeared as soon as the posse got too close" (Fetter and Fetter, 1979). The money was never recovered. Pictured in their fashionable derbies and vests are the "Wild Bunch": Harvey Logan (back left), Will Carver (back right), "The Sundance Kid," alias Harry Longbaugh (front left), Ben Kilpatrick (front center), and Butch Cassidy, alias Robert Leroy Parker (front right). (Telluride Historical Museum)

Ames, Col, Aug 21 '83

Ames

During the 1880s the Telluride mining region grew steadily. What little flat ground could be found at lower evaluations quickly blossomed into small multicultural, mining-support communities. The muddy streets of mining camps like Ames (above), Rico, Ophir, Sawpit, and Placerville teemed with freight wagons and strings of heavily loaded animals bound for high-country mines. In 1885 Ames, located about five miles south of Telluride, was described in a popular tourists guide as, "a mining camp on the San Miguel River, where are located smelting works and about 200 people."

Shown here in 1883, Ames blossomed near a site that soon became a famous railroad loop (see Ophir Loop on page 69). The crude boardwalks allowed people to avoid the deep mud. Several false-front buildings, including a saloon, the Ames Hotel, and Baumbauch's Drive-In Livery Feed and Sale Stable border the muddy thoroughfare. In 1890 Ames provided the unlikely setting for a world's electrical engineering first (see Lucien Nunn on page 57). (J. Collier photo: Colorado Historical Society, Stephen Hart Library)

Waiting for the climb

Numerous early photographs featured loaded pack burros ready to begin their arduous climb to the high country mines. This grouping of burros was gathered on Ames's main street, while men handling the wagon wait for the beasts of burden to move aside. Street maintenance still left something to be desired. One wonders about the profession of the woman peering from the second story window. (J. Collier photo: Denver Public Library, Western History Department)

Ore bags

Canvas ore bags are slung across the backs of the two burros closest to the camera. Packing trail animals constituted an art that not everyone could master. Preserved in ice, this battered ore bag remained intact in a high basin above Telluride. The back of the bag was worn smooth from rubbing on the burros' sides. (Author's photo: Author's collection)

Rico

In the late 1880s the mining camp of Rico, south of Lizard Head Pass, grew faster than any other camp in the region, including Telluride. "Seat of Dolores County, [Rico] is a mining town of much promise. It is situated on the east fork of the Dolores River, in a beautiful little valley, at the junction of Silver Creek, 35 miles from Silverton — "as the bird would fly" [and about equidistant from Telluride]. Population, 1,500. Altitude, 8,653 feet [a modern highway sign shows elevation as 8,827 feet]. Rico has two banks, stores, hotels, restaurants, and saloons of all kinds, with churches and schools, together with four smelting works" (*Grip-Sack Guide of Colorado (1885))*. In this panorama of Rico the photographer superimposed the names and locations of the mines above the town. Several of the mine names shown here are incorrect. (Colorado Historical Society, Stephen Hart Library)

Rails to Rico

Rio Grande Southern tracks reached Rico on October 15, 1891, adding strength to its already robust economy. A thin line of Rio Grande Southern rolling stock can be seen between the tips of the evergreens in the foreground of this crisp panorama. Taken only a few years after the panorama above, this image graphically documents the depletion of the forests near Rico. (Colorado Historical Society, Stephen Hart Library)

CHAPTER ONE: THE EARLY YEARS (1860S-1880S)

Serious competitions

Rico citizens took pride in their fire department — their best protection against the constant threat of a devastating conflagration. Fire department competitions with nearby camps included timed events — the stuff of high drama — with men, horses, and equipment pitted against one another. Hundreds of ardent supporters lined the streets to cheer their teams. The winners received accolades akin to modern cities' successful sports franchises all rolled into one. Losers went back to lick their wounds and practice. The men in this scene are about to showcase their speed and skill along Glasgow Avenue in downtown Rico.

In the background, J. B. Burley & Company's dry goods store stands next to the two-story Rico State Bank. A little farther down the main street (not shown here) Rico's largest stone building, the Hotel Enterprise, filled to capacity during such fire department competitions. (Colorado Historical Society, Stephen Hart Library)

Taking a break

Yoked oxen rest before (or perhaps after) hauling their heavy loads into the high country. A small boy, Emil Baer, sitting on the boardwalk along the unusually quiet Glasgow Avenue, contemplates the animals' fate. "Businessmen were locating in Rico at this time [1890], building on choice lots along Glasgow Avenue. Louis Hart occupied the building formerly run by David & Raymond. . . . The largest building in Rico, the new Hotel Enterprise, occupied three lots — the last building visible in this view" (McCoy, Collman, and Graves, 1996). (Denver Public Library, Western History Department)

Rico's premier mine

Many a bull train hauled tons of provisions to the Enterprise Mine above Rico. This prosperous mine soon had its own smelter, so these bull trains often started their descent burdened with an even heavier load: metal bullion. Beyond the smelter in the foreground are bunkhouses and a boardinghouse with a large kitchen and a general eating area. It is not hard to imagine that the hearty young men who labored for several weeks straight in these spartan heights often dreamed of the company they would keep on their next trip to Rico.

In the late 1880s the Enterprise's rich silver fueled Rico's biggest boom ever. Not only did Rico's population skyrocket, the demand for goods in the town and at the mines outstripped the freighters' capability to deliver them in a timely fashion. (Colorado Historical Society, Stephen Hart Library)

CHAPTER ONE: THE EARLY YEARS (1860S-1880S)

Old Ophir

Located about seven miles south of Telluride, the small camp of Ophir
clings precariously to the steep, barren slopes of the San Juans. In 1885 a
contemporary reported that Ophir consisted of, "two stores, a hotel, one stamp
mill, and two arastras for working free gold ores. Population about 200. The loads
in the vicinity are numerous and rich" (*Grip-Sack Guide of Colorado (1885)*).

An arastra was a Spanish device for grinding ore by means of a heavy stone
dragged around upon a circular bed. A burro, lead by one arm of an upright shaft,
supplied the power for this ineffective mining apparatus. (Reprinted from
Telluride and San Miguel County, 1894)

Special Attention to Transient
Trade.

A First Class Hotel in Every
Respect.

SILVER MOUNTAIN HOUSE,

....MRS. A. BONNER, Proprietress....

Rates Moderate. Tables Supplied with the Best the Market
affords. Finely Furnished Rooms, and Excellent Accommodations. Table Board by the Week.

OPHIR, COLO., *Jan. 8* _____ 189 *8*

Mrs. H. Adcott

Dangerous boardwalks

In this view old Ophir appears to be deserted, except for a lone rider on Granite Avenue. Closer inspection of the photograph, however, reveals three men staring at the camera from the Billiard Hall in the right foreground, while across the dirt main street a mounted man tends a group of burros. In the right background several men are gathered in front of a large false-front building. Farther down Granite Avenue, several barely distinguishable figures negotiate the step-like, dangerous boardwalks. Late at night, after an evening of drinking and entertainment, many an imbiber tumbled off the walkways. (Colorado Historical Society, Stephen Hart Library)

"A First Class Hotel in Every Respect"

In 1891, when the Rio Grande Southern laid its track several miles west of the original Ophir, many of the small camp's businesses migrated toward the depot. By the late 1890s booming Ophir claimed its own newspaper, *The Ophir Mail*, a fine school building, numerous businesses, and even a selection of fraternal orders — the Improved Order of the Red Men was the most popular. Ophir's Silver Mountain House claimed to be "A First Class Hotel In Every Respect." Its stationery (left) boasted of giving "Special Attention to Transient Trade." Presumably that meant catering to customers who traveled on the Rio Grande Southern. (Courtesy of Bill Ellicott)

Old Placerville

In the mid-1880s Placerville stood, "on the San Miguel river, west from Telluride, in the county seat. Population, about 100, most of whom are engaged in placer mining in the vicinity. Fare [via train and stagecoach] from Denver, $30.45" *(Grip-Sack Guide of Colorado (1885))*. Placerville, originally located at the confluence of the San Miguel and Dolores Rivers, also served as one of Dave Wood's way stations. Once the Rio Grande Southern reached

Placerville in the early 1890s, it became a major shipping point for cattle.

By the mid-1890s some of the businesses had moved to a higher tract of land about one mile south along the east side of the San Miguel River. They took the name of Placerville with them. This small mining and cattle community eventually claimed its own post office and several businesses. (Courtesy of P. David Smith)

WALTER EVANS, Postmaster.   ROBERT BERTIE, Asst. P. M.

PLACERVILLE, COLO.

CHAPTER ONE: THE EARLY YEARS (1860s-1880s)

A common problem with historical research

Frequently different descriptions and dates are found for the same image. For example, although all the descriptions place this photograph in Placerville, one has a choice of three different attributions. Choice one: "An old glass plate negative of two of Dave Wood's freighting teams on Crystal [Front] Street in the 1880s." Choice two: "Two families moving their belongings after the fire of 1913." Choice three: "Two of Dave Wood's freighting teams stopping for food and rest in the early 1900s." So which is it? Based on the older appearance of the buildings, the primitive condition of the road, and the lack of evidence of a railroad, the first choice seems the most logical. (Denver Public Library, Western History Department)

CHAPTER ONE: THE EARLY YEARS (1860s-1880s)

Hogs for the high country miners

Mountain communities like Telluride, Ames, Rico, Ophir, and Placerville depended on the mines for continued growth and prosperity. During the 1880s, before the railroad and most of the tramways, the mines depended on the freighters. Freighters literally brought everything to the mines, including frozen hogs (right) strapped to the backs of pack mules. The Smuggler-Union in Marshall Basin provides the backdrop.

The great high mines featured in the next chapter continued to rely on the freighters. But soon supplies from throughout Colorado and the United States rode all the way to Telluride on a spectacular narrow gauge railroad. With the coming of the Rio Grande Southern, more goods and equipment could be shipped in, and more ore and bullion could be shipped out. Nevertheless, the immediate economic future of the region looked dismal. The rising cost of energy — meaning the cost of wood and coal needed to heat the boilers that supplied power to the mines — was starting to eat up the majority of the mines' profits. A cheaper power supply for the mines had to be found or the entire San Juan Mining District faced financial disaster. (Courtesy of Walker Collection)

CHAPTER ONE: THE EARLY YEARS (1860S-1880S)

CHAPTER TWO
TELLURIDE THRIVES

This was Telluride's decade. The arrival of the Rio Grande Southern Railroad in 1890 signaled the start of Telluride's first sustained economic boom — it would wait nearly a century for another. More people, supplies, and mining equipment rode behind the smoke-and-cinder spewing engines that chugged their way over Dallas Divide. By 1891 the narrow gauge tracks extended south over rugged Lizard Head Pass to booming Rico. By early 1892 the first Rio Grande Southern train rolled into Durango. Now more ore from the San Miguel Mining District could be transported faster, easier, and cheaper to Durango's belching smelters.

Still, the boom would have fizzled were it not for the genius and pluck of a diminutive entrepreneur, Lucien Lucius Nunn. It is difficult to conceive how so little fame has accrued to Nunn, who catapulted Telluride and the San Juans into the age of electricity. In fact, during the early 1890s this Telluride resident formed the center of a scientific whirlwind that swept its way across Colorado, the United States, and the world.

Steam power had served the San Juan mining industry well until the mid-1880s when the adjacent forests began to disappear as miners cut many trees for fuel and for support timbers in the mine shafts. Incredibly, it was cheaper to have coal packed in by burros at forty to fifty dollars per ton than to transport wood from more distant locations. Several mines, particularly those located in remote regions, failed because of prohibitively high fuel costs. Even today a $2,500 monthly fuel bill would cause many mining operators to gasp. But Nunn had the answer. He decided to erect a high-voltage, alternating-current generating station at Ames (about five miles south of Telluride) by the gushing blue waters of the San Miguel River. Trouble was, this new untested phenomenon of alternating-current electricity had never been used for commercial purposes. Thomas Edison called the concept of alternating current splendid, but "utterly impractical." Nunn also had to work in the arctic zone of the San Juan Mountains under the severest of conditions. Nevertheless, as revealed in the historic photographs that follow, Nunn did it. He accomplished a scientific

(1890s)

and world's first: the use of alternating-current electricity for commercial power. Thus, with a flick of a switch at the small Ames power plant, Telluride mines became profitable again and the world had a new source of power.

Even in 1893, when the repeal of the Sherman Silver Purchase Act crippled many Colorado mining towns, including the mighty Leadville, the San Juan's "good drifts of gold ore" sustained Telluride. Between January 1895 and November 1896 the Tomboy Mine alone "took out $1,250,000, half of which was clear profit."

With a bustling population topping 2,500, Telluride exuded energy. For entertainment its citizens hosted fire department competitions that resulted in "world championship" times. Several new businesses, a brick schoolhouse (sporting the "world's first electrified school kitchen"), post office, banks, and the first-class Sheridan Hotel transformed Colorado Avenue into a bustling main street. One block south along East Pacific Avenue, dubbed "popcorn alley," vice still prevailed. The number of cribs increased and peace officer Jim Clarke died in an ambush near the San Juan Saloon.

Toward the end of the century Colonel Thomas Livermore of Boston formed a syndicate called the New England Exploration Company and bought the huge Smuggler-Union mining complex in Marshall Basin. In 1898 many of Telluride's young men marched off to fight in the Spanish-American war. During the last year of the 19th century the Liberty Bell, Smuggler-Union, and the Tomboy produced over $2,000,000 in ore.

But, trouble brewed. The miserable plight of the miners did not appear in the robust mining-production figures. Miners — near slaves — labored ten to twelve hours a day, seven days a week, in dangerous and appalling conditions. Local miners' unions were formed, including one in Telluride, to improve their lot. Unfortunately, these small and poorly organized groups seldom carried much clout. If one miner quit, or was fired for speaking out, another could always be found to take his place. When the powerful and militant Western Federation of Miners granted charter number sixty-three to the local Telluride union on July 28, 1896, it almost certainly signaled the coming of strikes and grief.

From mining camp to municipality

Above, snuggled beneath snow-covered peaks, Telluride awaits the coming of winter. In the foreground, Rio Grande Southern freight cars wait on sidetracks extending on both sides of the depot. Downtown, the San Miguel County Courthouse and Sheridan Hotel (originally owned by its namesake mining company) protrude over the roof of the American House on Colorado Avenue.

The year was 1890. As United States troops dismantled Fort Crawford south of Montrose, Colorado, mason workers in Telluride laid the first brick of the Sheridan Hotel. That same year 1,500 workers started construction of the Rio Grande Southern from Ridgway to Telluride. By November 23, 1891, the first locomotive chugged into the bustling camp, signalling the beginning of a prosperous decade. (Reprinted from *Telluride and San Miguel County*, 1894)

OFFICERS AND DIRECTORS OF THE TELLURIDE BOARD OF TRADE

E. L. DAVIS.

A. M. WRENCH.

R. S. ROBSON

N. T. MANSFIELD

CHAS. F. PAINTER

CHAS. S. WATSON.

A. M. READ.

R. J. CARSON.

Stalwarts of the business community

Precursor to the chamber of commerce, Telluride's Board of Trade unabashedly championed business growth. A booklet which promoted Telluride featured photographs of its board members (above). It was issued "for gratuitous distribution" and dedicated to "thoughtful and intelligent readers wherever they may be found." (Reprinted from *Telluride and San Miguel County*, 1894)

CHAPTER TWO: TELLURIDE THRIVES (1890s)

An unusual bandstand

In 1890 Telluride had "ninety business houses containing two hardware stores, blacksmith shops, jewelry stores, planning mills and photographic galleries, three boot and shoe stores, drug stores, grocery stores, livery stables and barber and bath shops; a paint shop, millinery store, fruit and confectionery store, furniture store, feed store and a brewery; seven laundries, and eleven saloons. There are five lawyers, four doctors, three dentists, two surveyors, two assayers and one insurance man" (quote unattributed). The town's flagpole in the middle of Colorado Avenue sported a "one-of-a-kind" raised, circular band platform. (Courtesy of P. David Smith)

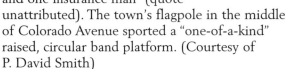

The high price of fuel

Steam power had served the San Juan mining industry well, until the mid-1880s when the adjacent forests began to disappear as miners cut thousands of trees for fuel, lumber, and the mines. It became cheaper to have coal packed in by burros at forty to fifty dollars per ton than to transport wood from more distant locations. Steam-powered contraptions like the one shown here became expensive to operate, as did the huge boilers at the mines. Imagine a monthly fuel bill — even now — of $2,500. Many of the mines located in remote regions failed because of the prohibitively high fuel costs. Indeed, profits at most mines in the region nosedived. (Telluride Historical Museum)

Lucien Lucius Nunn

Successful, tormented, and largely ignored by history, Lucien Lucius Nunn cut a formidable path through Telluride history. He also almost single-handedly saved the San Juan region's mining industry.

Reared on a farm in Ohio, he entered the Cleveland Academy at the age of fifteen. Nunn's collegiate career began with a brief and informal sojourn to study law at Leipzig and Goettingen Universities in Germany. He returned to the United States for further study in a Boston law office and attended an occasional lecture at Harvard Law School in 1879. Attracted by visions of wealth in the West, he arrived in Leadville, Colorado, like thousands of others, in 1880. (H. Reid photo: Courtesy of Arlene Reid)

The way to Telluride

Nunn's brief stint in Leadville, Colorado, was not successful. The Pacific Grotto Restaurant he opened in the rear of the most prominent gambling house in town failed. He decided to settle in Tombstone, Arizona. But threats of Indian hostilities in

Tombstone changed his mind. Instead, he moved to Durango, Colorado, where he opened another Pacific Grotto Restaurant. Once again Nunn's efforts as a connoisseur restauranteur floundered.

So in 1881, in his twenty-eighth year, he disconsolately arrived in Telluride. But this time he succeeded. Despite his tiny five-feet-one-inch frame, he had also done considerable construction and fine carpentry work in Leadville and Durango. Drawing upon his exemplary carpentry work, considerable law skills, and Napoleonic drive, he pushed himself to the top of the Telluride business world by 1888. His bachelor mansion with a fine study and zinc-lined bathtub

was the largest in town. A sixteen-stall stable held his favorite steeds which he expertly rode. Two guest homes made visitors comfortable.

By 1890 Nunn held controlling interest, with William Story, in the only bank in San Miguel County, three of the best store buildings on Colorado Avenue, and small interests in several mines, including the Gold King situated south of Telluride above Alta Lakes. But soon Nunn, like other mine owners in the region, began to fret over the high cost of fuel. Nunn, however, decided to do something about it. (Telluride Historical Museum) (Reprinted from *Telluride and San Miguel County*, 1894)

CHAPTER TWO: TELLURIDE THRIVES (1890s)

An untested electrical phenomenon

Today alternating current is a familiar electrical concept. But in 1890, when Nunn decided to erect a high-voltage alternating-current generating station at Ames (left), about five miles south of Telluride and three miles below the confluence of the Howard's Fork and the Lake Fork of the San Miguel River, few people had ever heard of it. In fact, with two notable exceptions — Nikola Tesla who had conceived of alternating current and George Westinghouse who was impressed by this young Croatian touched with genius — no one had faith in it. Further, this untested electric phenomenon had never been used for commercial purposes. Thomas Edison called the concept of alternating current splendid, but "utterly impractical." Nunn disagreed. He felt this odd-sounding phenomenon of "alternating current" held the key to solving the region's exorbitantly high fuel costs. (Colorado Historical Society, Stephen Hart Library)

A letter to his brother

Theoretical arguments about newfangled electricity held little concern for average Telluride residents, except for one person, Lucien Nunn. He believed it held the key to saving the mining industry. Exactly how Nunn knew is not known. His biographer, Stephan A. Bailey (1933), recorded that on May 21, 1890, Nunn wrote to his brother Paul:

> "The second matter of importance is that I wish you would investigate the subject of transmission of power by electricity. I have surveyors now at work laying out a line over the mountains . . . I am not sure of putting in the plant, but if I do I want you to take charge of the construction, and not let any one know that you are not an old hand at the work. Post yourself thoroughly and know whom to send for as an assistant if necessary. The mills have cost over $100,000 and of course the power to run them must be sure. It now costs upwards of $2500 per month for power, and I believe it can be furnished when the plant is up for $500."

(Quoted in Bailey, 67 - 68)

HISTORIC TELLURIDE IN RARE PHOTOGRAPHS

Pelton wheels for power

Rushing water from the San Miguel River was diverted into hoses in the small, crude power station. There it came blasting out of small nozzles, supplying the power to turn two six-foot-diameter Pelton water wheels belted to a Westinghouse generator. The original wheel installed in 1890 looked similar to this "1,200 horsepower wheel" installed in 1915. (Fort Lewis College, Center of Southwest Studies)

The very fiber of human culture

The familiarity with which we perceive electricity understandably detracts from an appreciation for its controversial development and use in America during the 1880s and 1890s. Few other eras in history have been privileged to see the birth and maturation of a phenomenon — electricity — which was to affect the very fiber of human culture. And all this in tiny Ames, Colorado.

Under the careful supervision of Paul Nunn, a new Westinghouse single-phase generator (above), primitive by today's standards, and an experimental motor designed by Tesla were finally in place as the winter of 1890-91 reached its frigid peak. Two transmission lines of bare copper wire were strung for almost three miles from the floor of the valley to the 12,000 foot

altitude of the Gold King Mine. Porcelain insulators atop Western Union cross-arms held the wire. The $700 cost was one percent of the construction cost of a direct-current line. In early spring of 1891, when Nunn was thirty-seven years old, all was ready. (Fort Lewis College, Center of Southwest Studies)

Power in the mountains

The farmers and ranchers who lived downstream from the Ames plant worried about the pending start-up. "Essences" and "life forces" of the stream, they claimed, would be sucked from the water, its salubrious strength compromised. In an era when transportation and speed were judged against the standard of a good mule or a fast horse, supplying power in alternating directions in mysterious copper lines at 186,000 miles per second was simply too much for them to accept.

Suddenly, or so it seemed after such colossal investments of time, energy, and hopes, Nunn threw the switch. Those present, no doubt, gasped and jumped back as a brilliant arc shot six feet into the air. In less time than a blink of an eye the Gold King (above) had electrical power to operate hoists and ore crushers; economical power that was to prove the salvation of the mining industry and transform the commercial application of electricity forever. (Reprinted from *Telluride and San Miguel County*, 1894)

Up and running, but the miners did not profit financially

The system ran flawlessly for thirty days. Paul Nunn admitted many years later that they were hesitant to shut it down for fear it could not be started again. His fears were misplaced. The system was easy to start. A simple starting motor cranked by hand proved effective time after time.

Mine owners profited the most in the short run. The Gold King's cost of operating machinery fell from approximately $2,500 to $500 a month. Other mines also found fiscal salvation. In 1890 the Revenue, located near Ouray, had just finished a costly new direct-current power station about eight miles from their main tunnels. They abandoned it almost immediately because it was actually cheaper to string ten miles of wire over 13,000-foot Imogene Pass and dip into Nunn's economic reservoir of high-voltage alternating current.

In a few years Nunn became so busy with alternating-current projects in Utah that he leased the Gold King to J. K. McCoy. This receipt (above) shows that McCoy paid one of his Gold King miners, W. Daily, $3.00 a day. After deductions for board, store, and insurance Daily pocketed only $50 for a month's work. (Author's collection)

The towns people benefited

Townspeople also profited from Nunn's successes. After Nunn's alternating-current reached Telluride in 1894, there was a warmer and safer feeling about life in general with well-lighted streets, well-lighted homes, and the long-term prospect of a cheap and reliable source of power and light. In this early photograph a group of men, probably including Nunn, pose beside one of the power poles that soon spread Nunn's alternating current throughout Telluride.

Nunn soon built other stations in other states. In 1897 he completed one in Provo Canyon, Utah. From 1902 to 1910 Lucien and Paul Nunn designed and constructed one of the largest single hydroelectric stations in the world for the Ontario Power Company at Niagara Falls. This hard work paid dividends as Lucien Nunn amassed an even larger fortune. (Fort Lewis College, Center of Southwest Studies)

CHAPTER TWO: TELLURIDE THRIVES (1890s)

The Telluride Power Transmission Company.

CAPITAL $15.000.000.

L.L.NUNN, GENERAL MANAGER.

TELLURIDE, COLO.

A bureaucratic nightmare

Organizing and orchestrating the continued smooth operation and expansion of the Ames power station was a bureaucratic nightmare. An inspection of the early correspondence and records available in the Center of Southwest Studies at Fort Lewis College in Durango, Colorado, substantiates this. A constant flurry of letters and telegrams — thousands of them — spanning over three decades passed between Nunn and his suppliers, supporters, and detractors. Ultimately this took its toll on Nunn.

On April 2, 1925, the life of Lucien Nunn, with some professional and even less public recognition, drew quietly to a close. Yet to this day untold millions who unthinkingly flick on their power and light switches owe Nunn some small gratitude. (Courtesy of Bill Ellicott)

The Rio Grande Southern Railroad

Prosperity also came to Telluride on the rails of the Rio Grande Southern in 1891. People and supplies could be hauled in and out more quickly and less expensively. Most importantly, ore from the San Miguel Mining District could be transported faster and cheaper to Durango's belching smelters. "The Rio Grande Southern [RGS] had the distinction of being the last major narrow-gauge railroad to be constructed in Colorado, starting in 1890 — 100 years ago this year [1990]. RGS mainline track twisted and turned for 162 awesome miles, traversing some of Colorado's most spectacular scenic mountain formations before reaching Durango, at the southern end of the line" (Collman and McCoy, 1990). In this classic photograph elk antlers add a Western touch to RGS engine 203. (Telluride Historical Museum)

Otto Mears

An RGS locomotive puffs its way over Dallas Divide. The one name that will always be synonymous with the construction of the Rio Grande Southern is Russian-born Otto Mears. "By 1889 Mears had connected much of southwestern Colorado with his roads. Included in his accomplishments was the spectacular road from Ouray to Silverton via Red Mountain, much of which was cut out of the solid rock of the Uncompahgre Canyon. On October 30 he formed the Rio Grande Southern Railroad with a group of prominent citizens that included the governor, and he set his sights on a project that would reach Telluride. The railroad was to be narrow-gauge, and the work would be done by the Rio Grande Southern Construction Company. To finance the venture Mears sold a total of $9,020,000 worth of stocks and bonds in the company. Telluride in fact would be but part of a great line that ran down through Rico, Dolores, and Mancos, to connect Ridgway with Durango" (Fetter and Fetter, 1979). (H. Reid photo: Courtesy of Arlene Reid)

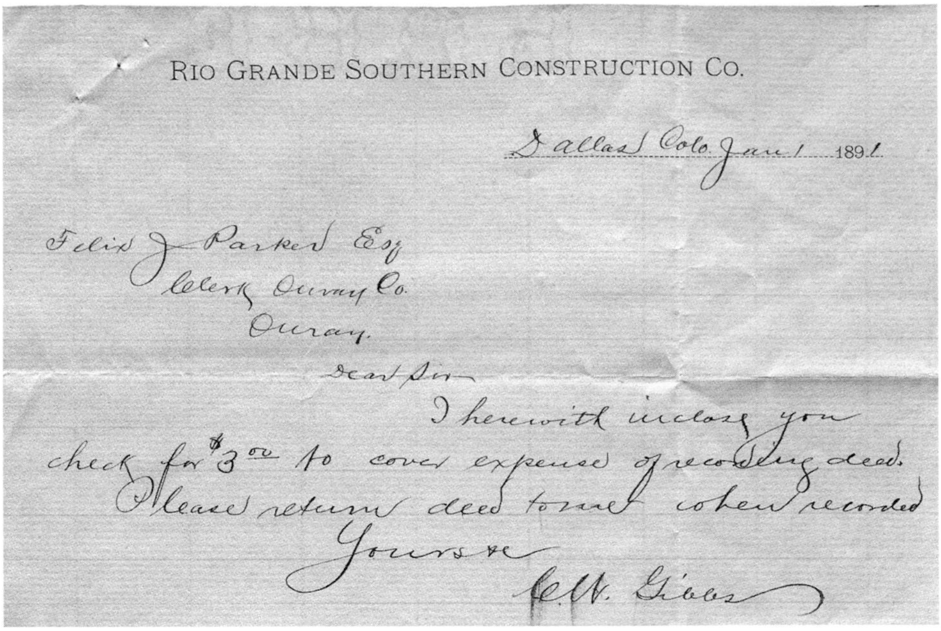

RIO GRANDE SOUTHERN CONSTRUCTION CO.

Dallas, Colo. Jan. 1, 1891

Felix J. Parker Esq
Clerk Ouray Co.
Ouray.

Dear Sir

I herewith inclose you check for $3.00 to cover expense of recording deed. Please return deed to me when recorded

Yours &c
C.W. Gibbs

Paperwork

Shown here is a rare piece of "Rio Grande Southern Construction Co." stationery from Dallas and an equally scarce leasing bill paid to the Denver and Rio Grande Railroad for use of its terminal facilities at Ridgway. Reams of paperwork accompanied the construction and operation of railroads. Bottles of Carter's ink and Schaffer pens were integral fixtures in all Rio Grande Southern depots. (Both courtesy of P. David Smith)

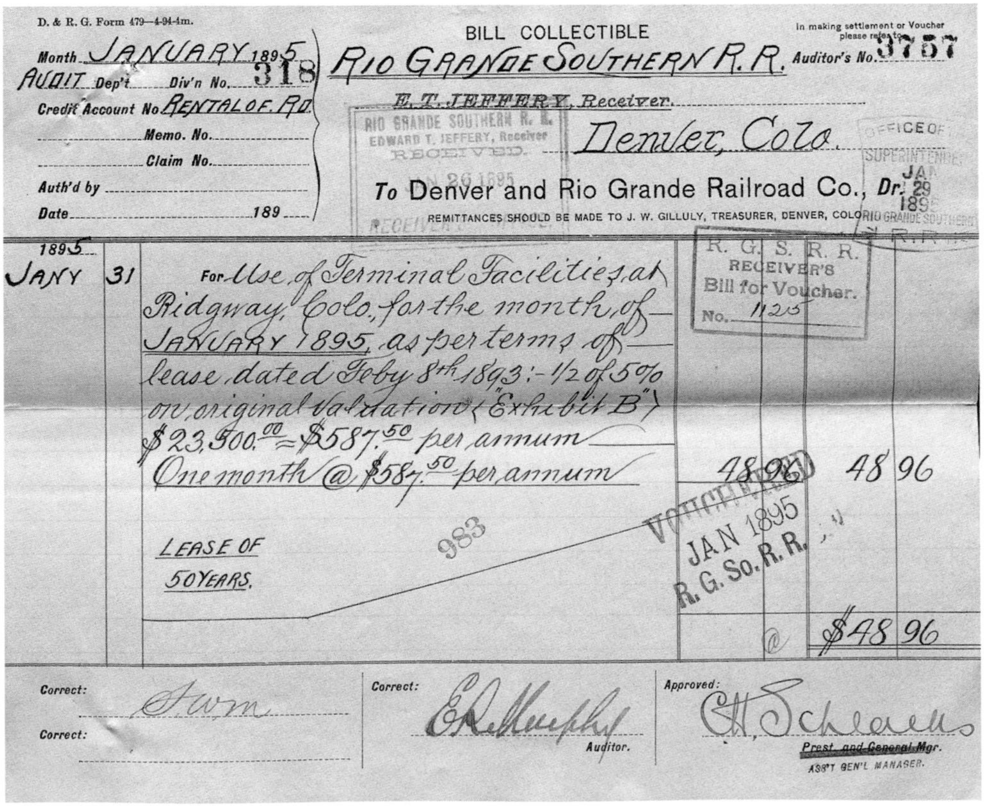

CHAPTER TWO: TELLURIDE THRIVES (1890s)

Atop Dallas Divide

The RGS crossed the lowest portion of the Uncompahgre Plateau at a place called Dallas Divide [above], 8,989 feet in elevation. The steepest grades along the mainline were encountered on the northern side of Dallas Divide. . . . This part of the railroad proved to be a locomotive engineer's nightmare, resulting in magnificent wrecks, and great skill was required of the crews to handle heavy tonnage downgrade — not to mention the involvement of additional engines used as helpers to haul the tonnage upgrade" (Collman and McCoy, 1990).

Pictured here in more recent times is RGS engine No. 455 idling at Dallas Divide. Perhaps the snowplow was needed for negotiating Lizard Head Pass between Telluride and Rico. A two-story ranch house is nestled near the edge of the aspen grove toward the left-center of the image. Remnants of this structure can still be seen. (Courtesy of P. David Smith)

CHAPTER TWO: TELLURIDE THRIVES (1890s)

A different mode of transportation

With the coming of the Rio Grande Southern, Dave Wood's vignette (above) featuring stage and freight stock soon gave way, figuratively and literally, to the steam engine vignette on this stock certificate (right). (Courtesy of Bill Ellicott) (Courtesy of P. David Smith)

Ophir Loop

The Ophir Loop between Telluride and Rico ranks among the premier railroad building feats of the late 19th century. An awed contemporary wrote: "The difficulties of mountain ascent surmounted and overcome by engineering skill so that a path is made for the puffing steam engine to pull its trail of commerce up the rugged, almost perpendicular, sides and over their summits, has in Ophir Loop a marvelous exhibition. To see it is to be confounded and enchanted by its magnificent grandeur, and marvelous confirmation of the triumphs of engineering skill in this our day and generation. The illustration [left] which accompanies this article is but a faint expression of what you must realize by a trip over the Loop by rail" (*Telluride and San Miguel County*, 1894). (W. H. Jackson photo: Reprinted from *Telluride and San Miguel County*, 1894)

H
I
S
T
O
R
I
C

T
E
L
L
U
R
I
D
E

I
N

R
A
R
E

P
H
O
T
O
G
R
A
P
H
S

Below Lizard Head Pass

A closer view of Ophir Loop shows the start of the Rio Grande Southern's breath-taking ascent to the summit of Lizard Head Pass. (Courtesy of Walker Collection)

"R. G. SO. Ry." brass baggage tag

Passengers who checked their bags received a numbered brass tag to match the one put on their luggage. This scarce Rio Grande Southern tag surfaced near Vance Junction. The damage indicates that it may have been in a baggage car derailed during a flood in 1909. (Author's photo: Courtesy of Bill Ellicott)

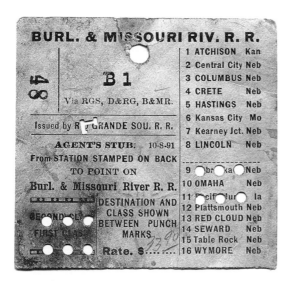

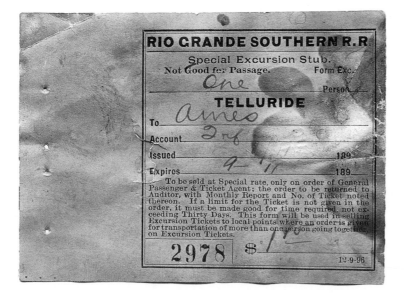

Railroad links

During the last quarter of the 19th century various railroad systems' tentacles stretched rapidly across the West, often linking with one another. As witnessed by these well-worn ticket stubs from the 1890s — all back-stamped with "Rio Grande Southern R. R., Telluride, Colo." — passengers from Telluride often bought tickets from other connecting railroads. The ticket on the left is a Rio Grande Southern ticket from Telluride to Ames for a fare of $1.15. (Courtesy of David E. Kuhlemeier)

Lizard Head Pass in winter

The distinctive rock formation jutting up in the center of this scene gave Lizard Head Pass its name. Imagine riding the rails over this pass between Telluride and Rico during the winter. On crisp, clear days the sheer beauty of such a setting awed passengers. During howling snowstorms that nearly buried stalled trains, passengers surely cursed this same gorgeous setting. (Courtesy of P. David Smith) (A.E. Buys photo: Author's collection)

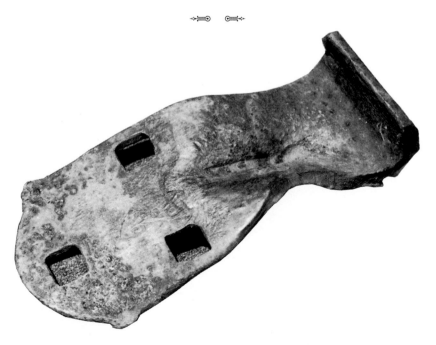

CHAPTER TWO: TELLURIDE THRIVES (1890S)

Nauman & Courtney, *Telluride, Colo.*

Images for posterity

Early photographers bequeathed to history many lasting images of early Telluride. The "Nauman and Courtney" studio snapped this uncommon photograph of two Plains Indians. Bells sewn on the leggings of the man on the left indicate that they belonged to a dance troop. (Courtesy of Bill Mahoney)

Cardboard backing

To prevent early photographic paper from curling, it was usually glued to a piece of cardboard slightly larger than the photograph itself. Telluride photographer W. J. Carpenter advertised on his cardboard backing. (Courtesy of Joann and Wes Leech)

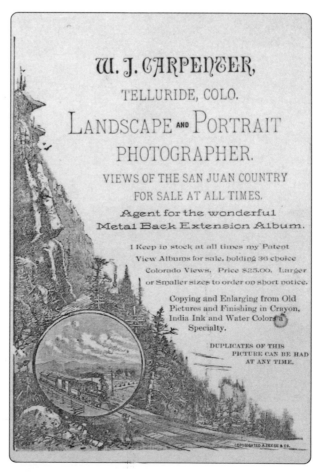

W. J. CARPENTER,
TELLURIDE, COLO.
LANDSCAPE AND PORTRAIT
PHOTOGRAPHER.
VIEWS OF THE SAN JUAN COUNTRY
FOR SALE AT ALL TIMES.
Agent for the wonderful
Metal Back Extension Album.

I keep in stock at all times my Patent
View Albums for sale, holding 36 choice
Colorado Views, Price $25.00. Larger
or Smaller sizes to order on short notice.

Copying and Enlarging from Old
Pictures and Finishing in Crayon,
India Ink and Water Colors a
Specialty.

DUPLICATES OF THIS
PICTURE CAN BE HAD
AT ANY TIME.

A morning on Colorado Avenue

Here Carpenter photographed a group of pack burros loaded with wooden crates. The Rio Grande Southern cut into the long haul business of freighters like Dave Wood (perhaps the one in the suit at left center), but not the short haul. Rather, the railroads transferred the supplies directly to freight teams waiting at the Telluride depot. From there beasts of burden transported the goods to where no railroad could go — the high country mines.

Carpenter also captured masons on scaffolding (right center) constructing the First National Bank building and adding a third story to the New Sheridan Hotel (directly beneath tower). Notice, too, the sign (right foreground) for the San Juan Hardware Co. Today, fully automatic cameras make it easy to forget how difficult it was to take photographs in the late 19th century. (W. J. Carpenter photo: Denver Public Library, Western History Department)

A distinctive Telluride landmark

Constructed of sandstone from a quarry on Cornet Creek, the First National Bank's distinctive corner tower graced the corner of Fir Street and Colorado Avenue well into the 20th century. Dual images of the venerable building appear on a stereocard (above) for the popular hand-held stereoscopic viewers. The bank's arched entry with elegant stained glass window panels greeted the customers. The tower has been dismantled. Later the building served as the headquarters for BPO Elks 692. (Colorado Historical Society, Stephen Hart Library)

An artist's rendition

A drawing on one of the First National Bank's checks gave the sandstone building a more imposing appearance. (Author's photo: Courtesy of Ralph Kemper)

Nunn, Wrench, and 1.5 percent interest

Photographs of two men whose names are on this receipt have already been featured. L. L. Nunn (see page 57) is listed as president of the First National Bank (formerly San Miguel County Bank) and A. M. Wrench (see page 55) is listed as the cashier. As for the banking business, "Interest was usually 1.5 percent a month, and no one bothered using pennies. If more than 2 1/2 cents was in question a nickel would be used; amounts less that 2 1/2 cents were forgotten" (Fetter and Fetter, 1979). (Courtesy of P. David Smith)

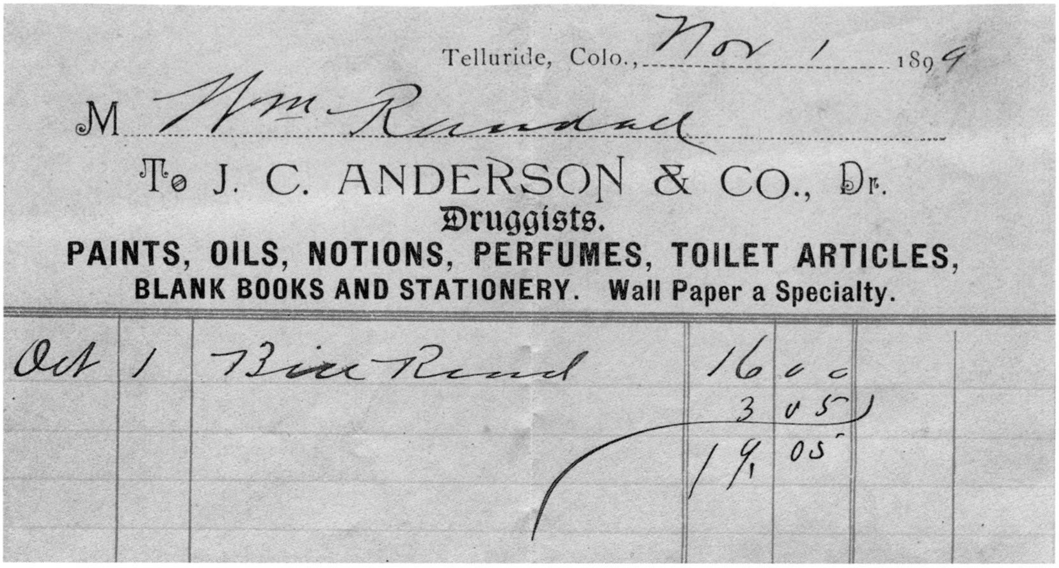

Telluride, Colo., Nov 1 1899

M Wm Randall

To J. C. ANDERSON & CO., Dr.

Druggists.

PAINTS, OILS, NOTIONS, PERFUMES, TOILET ARTICLES,

BLANK BOOKS AND STATIONERY. Wall Paper a Specialty.

Oct 1 Bill Rend 16 00

3 05

19 05

Drugstores, murder, and a prolific photographer

The building with an awning on North Fir Street and West Colorado Avenue, across from the First National Bank (previous page), housed a long line of Telluride druggists and jewelers, the Telluride Post Office, and a prolific photographer (Homer Reid). First came J. C. Anderson and Company Druggists (which housed the post office in back), followed by Anderson, Baisch and Company Druggists and Jewelers. Baisch, the co-owner of the store, "was murdered for his diamond ring when an angry miner claimed Baisch had swindled him by not paying enough for the miner's high-grade [stolen] ore" (Fetter and Fetter, 1979). The Bank of Telluride stood immediately east of the drugstore until it was demolished to make room for the new Mahr building.

More recently the H. C. Baisch Drugstore (owned by Frank Wilson) also housed Homer Reid's watch repair business. There Reid graciously shared his incredible collection of photographs with curious amateur historians and numerous railroad buffs. Tragically, in 1990 a fire claimed the landmark H. C. Baisch Drugstore building. Shown here are two receipts from the early drugstore and jewelry businesses. (Courtesy of P. David Smith) (Author's photo: Courtesy of Ralph Kemper)

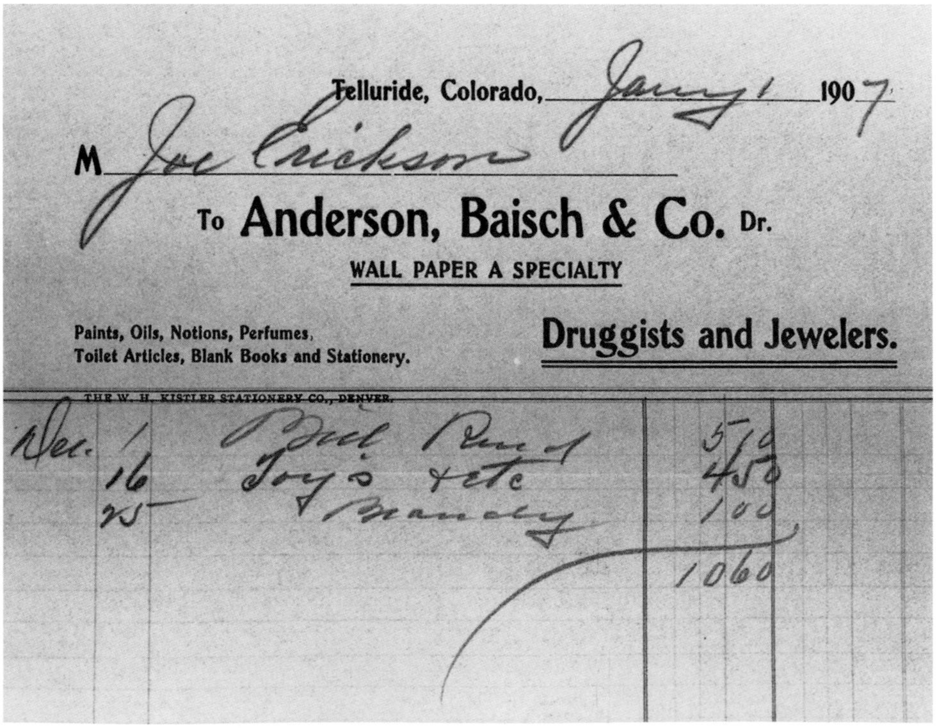

Telluride, Colorado, Jany 1 1907

M Joe Erickson

To Anderson, Baisch & Co. Dr.

WALL PAPER A SPECIALTY

Paints, Oils, Notions, Perfumes, Toilet Articles, Blank Books and Stationery.

Druggists and Jewelers.

THE W. H. KISTLER STATIONERY CO., DENVER.

Dec. 1 Bill Rend 5 00

16 Toys etc 4 50

25 Brace 1 00

10 00

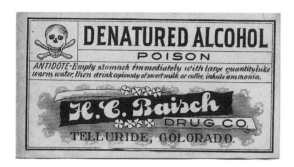

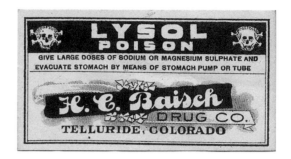

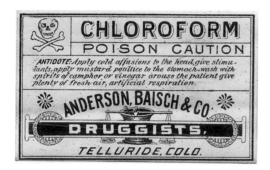

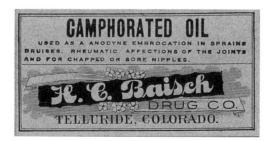

Paper labels

These original, stylish paper labels were affixed to pharmacy bottles from Anderson, Baisch and Company Druggists, and the H. C. Baisch Drug Company of Telluride. (All courtesy of Joann and Wes Leech)

The difference between life and death

Telluride firemen, probably volunteers, pose for a photograph in front of the American House on Colorado Avenue. An organized and efficient volunteer fire company often made the difference between life and death for hastily constructed mining camps. (Telluride Historical Museum) (A.E. Buys photos: Author's collection)

Fire chief

An unidentified Telluride fire chief stands erect with his fire trumpet. While rushing to fires, fireman blew these trumpets to alert the citizenry and clear the streets. Except during Fourth of July parades, no one wanted to hear the sounds of bleating fire trumpets and clanging bells. On this well-worn photograph, someone touched up the front piece on the chief's helmet. (Courtesy of Bill Mahoney)

Wet Test champions

Fourth of July celebrations inevitably found firemen from different mining towns competing against one another. Shown here on Colorado Avenue in front of the First National Bank, Telluride Hose Team No. 1 won the Wet Test contest for Southwestern Colorado on July 3, 1892.

These contests were more than entertainment. In the late 19th century fire departments constituted sources of community pride and pillars of defense against the ever present danger of a cataclysmic fire — especially in mining camps built primarily of wood. Indeed, a city with a championship hose cart team could take comfort in knowing that they had the best fire protection possible. (W. J. Carpenter photo: Denver Public Library, Western History Department)

New champions

In 1895 the Grand Junction Hose Cart Brigade — competing in Telluride — ran 100 yards "from a standing start," pulling 150 feet of hose while still on the run, "broke the line," coupled to a hydrant and "showed water at the tip," all in the world record time of 27 2/5 seconds. The elegant Telluride trophy cup still stands proudly on one of the Grand Junction Fire Department's display cases. The cup is engraved:

WET TEST AT TELLURIDE
JUNE 20TH 1895
TIME 27 2/5 SEC

"Presented, Grand Junction, Hose Company," is also engraved under the spout. (Author's photo: Courtesy of the Grand Junction Fire Department) (A.E. Buys photo: Author's collection)

Silver Cornet Band

Telluride townspeople took great pride in their award-winning brass band. Shown here parading west on Colorado Avenue with a dog leading the way, the uniformed Silver Cornet Band commanded the attention of the Fourth of July celebrants. A group of Masons marches close behind. Towering over Telluride are Ajax, Ingram, and Telluride Peaks. (Denver Public Library, Western History Department)

(43)-10647-Trailing timbers up to Tomboy mine (S.) near Telluride, Colo. Copyright Underwood & Underwood. U-118996

"Boundless possibilities"

Mining reigned in San Miguel County. All the San Juan camps, including Telluride, owed their existence to the mines above them. "This limited space forbids further mention of individual properties, but enough has been said to show that the mineral bearing area lying within the boundaries of San Miguel County contains many of the most extensively developed and best paying mines in the state. The future contains boundless possibilities."

These are only a few sentences that customers of Telluride's "The Cash Grocery" could read on the back of their receipts in 1894. The Board of Trade furnished the text.

On their way to the Tomboy, one of those "extensively developed and best paying mines," a train of burros (above) drag timber up the famous trail that also branched off to the Smuggler-Union, another huge mining complex. (Courtesy of Joann and Wes Leech)

Tomboy Gold Mining Company in summer and winter

"Just under the peak of the mountain ridge separating Ouray from San Miguel County, in Elephant Basin on Savage Fork of Marshall Creek, lie the properties known as the Belmont and Tomboy lode claims belonging to this company . . . being one of the largest and richest gold mines in the entire San Juan." Purchased in 1891 by a syndicate in Shanghai, China, the Far Eastern owners "proceeded to equip [sic] with a power and reduction plant. A large mill building was erected and fitted up with crusher, compound rolls, Huntington mills, vanners and bumping tables for concentration."

"The direct current electrical power has been abandoned as inefficient and in its stead is now being installed an alternating current plant that will be supplied with power by the San Miguel Consolidated. Additional ground is being opened up on the mines, and by the time this pamphlet is in the hands of the reader the mill will be running to its full capacity night and day." All the above quotes are from The Board of Trade's 1894 pamphlet, *Telluride and San Miguel County*, that should have included the following rubric: "Nunn's Power Plant at Ames Saves the Tomboy." In 1897 the Tomboy changed hands again, this time "when it was reported sold to Rothchilds' of London for $2,000,000" (Wolle, 1949). (Courtesy of Irene R. Visintin and Elvira F. Visintin Wunderlich) (Colorado Historical Society, Stephen Hart Library)

CHAPTER TWO: TELLURIDE THRIVES (1890s)

Comfortable community room

Acommunity room similar to this one (possibly the Telluride Club) in one of the Tomboy boardinghouses provided miners and their spouses with a place to socialize, listen to the piano, play cards (no gambling permitted), write letters, or read a book. With snow piled high several months a year, a toasty warm, nicely decorated community room provided a much needed refuge from the dank, cold mine and the harsh weather. (Telluride Historical Museum)

(44)-10648-Loads of gold coming down trail from Tomboy mine to Telluride, Colo. Copyright Underwood & Underwood. U-119002

CHAPTER TWO: TELLURIDE THRIVES (1890s)

Bars of gold

A group of smelter workers pose by a stack of gold bars, each one worth a small fortune in the 1890s. (Telluride Historical Museum)

Loads of gold

Loads of processed gold from the Tomboy rumble down the trail to Telluride (left). Fortunately for Telluride many of the mines yielded more gold than silver. Even in 1893, when the repeal of the Sherman Silver Purchase Act crippled many Colorado mining towns — including the mighty silver-based Leadville — the San Juan's "good drifts of gold ore" sustained Telluride. Between January 1895 and November 1896 the Tomboy Mine alone "took out $1,250,000, half of which was clear profit" (Lavender, 1987). (Denver Public Library, Western History Department)

The Smuggler-Union mills

66Within the area bounded on the north by Ouray County, on the east by San Juan County, on the south by Dolores County and on the west by Mt. Wilson, whose stern and rugged peak marks the termination of the Continental Divide in that direction is found the [w]orld famed Smuggler-Union property, from which since 1879 has been taken more than ten millions [sic] in gold and silver, and that in 1892 produced in gold alone — one-fiftieth — or two percent of the entire gold product of the United States. The property is developed by more than twenty miles of underground work in shafts, levels and tunnels. . . . In its many stopes, levels, up-raises and shafts 1,000 men could find employment, and it would require their constant labor for ten successive years to work out the ore now in sight" (*Telluride and San Miguel County*, 1894).

Pictured here is the Smuggler-Union mill complex tucked beneath Marshall Basin, almost two-thousand feet below the mines. Ingram Falls and Bridal Veil Falls highlight the magnificent mountain backdrop. (Courtesy of P. David Smith)

CHAPTER TWO: TELLURIDE THRIVES (1890S)

A lethal separation

Only a fraction of gold is found in the form of surface nuggets in the San Juans. Rather, the majority of gold is locked in hard ore. Numerous businesses (right) made a handsome profit manufacturing state-of-the-art mill equipment needed to extract the tiny flecks of gold from the ore.

First the ore had to be pulverized by crushers (above), then subsequently subjected to various processing methods that separated the gold from the ore before it emerged as a yellowish concentrate. "One method is the cyanide process. Fine particles of gold and silver are dissolved out of the pulp by a weak solution of deadly poisonous potassium or sodium cyanide [in vats like those shown below], filtered and then precipitated as an unappetizing black goo on zinc shavings or zinc dust — all of which sounds simpler than it actually is" (Lavender, 1943). This cyanide process, among others using equally deadly chemicals, has left a legacy of costly and controversial environmental cleanup programs. (Colorado Historical Society, Stephen H. Hart Library) (Author's photo: Author's collection) (Colorado Historical Society, Stephen H. Hart Library)

Dwarfed by the surroundings

A string of freight animals from the Smuggler-Union, dwarfed by the surroundings, snakes down the Marshall Basin trail. Long wooden snowsheds cover the entrance to the Penn Tunnel burrowed beneath Marshall Basin. Marshall Basin is located about four miles northeast of Telluride at altitudes between 11,500 and 12,500 feet. Between 1875 and 1876, the Mendota, Sheridan, Smuggler, and Union (later a part of the Smuggler) were staked close together in Marshall Basin. Indeed, a common vein ran beneath them. "This mineral deposit would turn out to be the largest vein in the district, about four to six feet wide. It was eventually worked for a length of four miles and to a depth of 3,000 feet. In the early years, this vein was called the Sheridan vein, but later, it was usually called the Smuggler-Union vein" (Collman and McCoy, 1991). (Courtesy of Walker Collection)

"That hanging road over so much empty space"

In the early 1890s freighters and their animals take a break to pose for the photographer on their way to the Smuggler-Union. Notice the men sitting nonchalantly on top of a large and cumbersome boiler, while another man stands beside a piece of wheeled machinery being dragged by plow horses.

Lest one get the impression from this photograph that negotiating this trail was easy, read the words of Muriel Wolle, well-known chronicler of Colorado mining history in the 1940s: "The road [lower Tomboy and Smuggler trail] was literally hung to the cliff, which swept down hundreds of feet to the New Smuggler mill at Pandora. To go ahead was terrifying, to look below sickening. For the first time in my 'mining career' I lost my nerve as I thought of driving out onto that hanging road over so much empty space . . . " (Wolle, 1949). (Reprinted from *Telluride and San Miguel County*, 1894)

Black powder, dynamite, and blasting caps

Most miners described black powder as dangerous, loud, and smoky. In this photograph heavily burdened pack mules freight the cumbersome explosive up Marshall Basin trail to the Smuggler-Union Mine. Without black powder, boring tunnels and mine shafts would have been far more difficult and prohibitively expensive.

Years later mules and burros hauled safer (relatively speaking), more powerful sticks of dynamite in wooden crates, some of which featured Indian motifs (above left). Blasting caps used to ignite the dynamite came in small metal tins like the one shown here (above right). (Author's photos: Author's collection) (Courtesy of Walker Collection)

CHAPTER TWO: TELLURIDE THRIVES (1890s)

A sloppy survey

"It was not until the Smuggler was located [September 1876] that the vein began to have a reputation. This location was made by J. B. Ingram, and was situated between the Sheridan and the Union whose boundary stakes had been set out to cover more than the 1,500 feet of ground each. Very high grade ore was struck on the surface of the Smuggler and shipping began. The difficulties of transportation were great, it being necessary to first pack by burro train to Ouray, and then to ship by wagon, 260 miles, to the end of the railroad. Moreover, fully six months in the year the mine was inaccessible to pack trains" (*Telluride and San Miguel County*, 1894).

According to local legend, serendipity made Ingram rich. Excited to discover that the rich Sheridan and the Union mining claims exceeded their legally allotted 500' x 1,500', he immediately rode to Silverton to file a claim on the portion of the old mining allotments that exceeded their boundaries. He boldly named his claim "The Smuggler," which is shown above in later years. (Courtesy of Walker Collection)

Loading the ore in the early days

A scarce photograph shows how early miners in the San Juan region, including those working the Smuggler-Union, loaded ore into waiting freight wagons. This scene also depicts the method employed for transporting ore down the mountain prior to the construction of the Smuggler tramway. (Denver Public Library, Western History Department)

CHAPTER TWO: TELLURIDE THRIVES (1890s)

Smuggler Mine
Boarding & Apartment Houses

Living on the edge

The Smuggler's boardinghouse with its spacious porch can be seen above the Bullion Tunnel, the main access to the rich Smuggler vein. By the 1890s the Smuggler-Union (and the Tomboy) looked like small cities in the sky. They had enough living accommodations and shelters to keep operating all winter. Historian David Lavender wrote: "Hundreds of men lived in bunkhouses and ate well in the boardinghouse." Mining companies knew that good food helped reduce turnover rates. (Courtesy of Walker Collection)

Time to eat

One of the Smuggler's well-lit dining rooms stands ready for ravenously hungry miners. A large Smuggler Mine Company monogram can be distinguished on one of the ceiling support timbers by the kitchen entrance. (Telluride Historical Museum)

Poor pay, long shifts, and hard play

Between shifts miners from the Smuggler-Union stare intently into the camera's lens. Note that some of them — mostly young men — have mining candles protruding from their pockets even though electrical power and lights had long been a fixture at the mine. For three dollars a day, minus a dollar for boarding, they worked ten-hour shifts, day and night. "At the close of the Saturday day shift, workers who were free could go to town, if they wished, and enjoy Telluride's numerous and obliging fleshpots. Orders for riding horses were sent to the packers, who led the saddled animals up on that day's trip. The miners whipped the rented mounts back down the hill at a faster pace than was always safe. Late on Sunday they rode back with their hangovers" (Lavender, 1987). (Courtesy of Walker Collection)

Chapter Two: Telluride Thrives (1890s)

The company store

If the miners needed to buy something they could wait until the weekends to go to town or they could purchase it at the company store. Because of their low wages, miners often found themselves in debt to the companies that employed them. It was a vicious fiscal cycle.

A store at the Smuggler Mine under the management of "Laughlin & Kuskey" issued their own tokens. An old corroded token once used in exchange for merchandise, is shown above. The bottom rim of the token is embossed "Smuggler, Colo." The Smuggler also had its own post office. (Author's photo: Courtesy of Bill Ellicott)

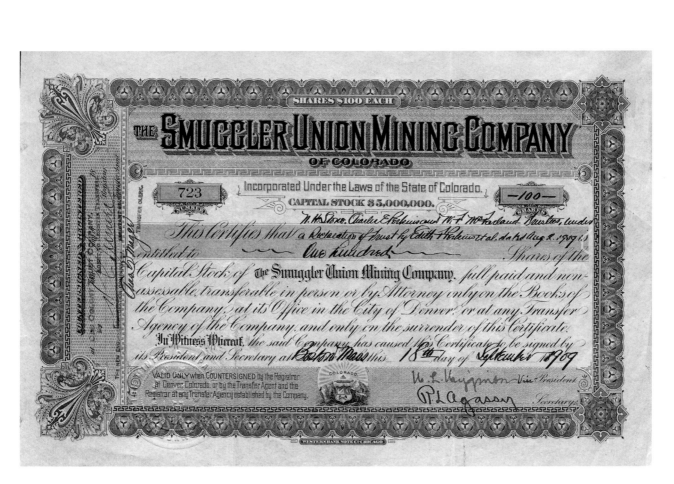

"Big money people"

Even though they risked their lives daily, few miners owned even a single share of stock in the companies. "Big money people" from back East held most of the shares like the one shown above. Moreover, only the shareholders and owners profited from the miners' hard work. (Courtesy of P. David Smith)

"How did they haul all this cable up here?"

A question asked incredulously by hikers in the high San Juans who encounter long lengths of rusting tram cable snaking across steep boulder fields, dangling hundreds of feet over vertical ledges, or swaying off high ridges. In some basins, enough of this thick iron cable remains to form colossal metal spider webs weighing thousands of pounds.

How did they haul all this cable up there? An extraordinary photograph (above) taken during the summer of 1897 provides the answer. Here fifty-two of Dave Wood's mules are connected by 10,810 feet of cable — without splices — weighing approximately 17,000 pounds. In unison they trudged up the treacherous mountain trails with their collective burdens. For anyone who has struggled to simply hike up these small trails, such a feat is almost impossible to imagine. (Moore Brothers photo: Courtesy of Barb Muntyan)

Transporting the cable

From his horse Dave Wood carefully watches the beginning of his cable-connected mule train's legendary trek to the Nellie Mine perched 11,190 feet above sea level. Wood claimed a mule was "the only animal for a job like this because, burros were to [sic] dinky and horses to [sic] flighty." Nevertheless, "One slip — one mule lost — and the whole train could be lost. But these were men who planned to avoid that first lost mule, and they got the train safely to the mine. The feat is still a favorite story of old-timer yarnsters in Telluride" (Wood and Wood, 1977). (Courtesy of Dorothy H. Evans)

Overlooked and underappreciated

Freighters were often justifiably described as the life lines of the mines. Yet one seldom reads about another, equally vital means of conveyance: tramways. Also called "aerial tramways," or simply "trams," these marvels of engineering merit a prominent place in mining history.

Snow encroaches on a pair of wooden towers along the lower portion of a staggering 6,700 foot tram constructed from the Smuggler-Union mill in Pandora to the Smuggler-Union Mine almost 3,000 vertical feet above. "The upper cable (at the top of the towers) was a fixed cable. The buckets were fitted with a frame and wheels, which rode on this fixed cable. The lower cable was the moving cable and pulled the ore buckets" (Collman and McCoy, 1991). This part of the tram joined the Smuggler-Union's Penn Tunnel (the white buildings in the upper background) with the giant mill below. Later one needed a ticket to ride the Smuggler tramway. (Courtesy of Walker Collection) (Courtesy of Bill Mahoney)

Nearly a triple fatality

A few trams continued to operate into the 1950s. After World War II the Mahoney brothers, Bill and Pat "Posse," worked at the Penn Tunnel (its tram and tram entrance shown here.) Bill worked as a loader and Posse as a blacksmith. One night, after their shift ended at 2:00 a.m., they climbed into one of the buckets for a ride down to Pandora (inset). Another loader, Harold Porterfield, was already in the bucket. Somehow the brakeman, who operated the tram "missed the grip," — a device that attaches the bucket to the moving cable. Instantly the bucket started gaining momentum as it headed — unattached — down the steep tramway. At first Bill and Posse tried to slow the bucket by grabbing onto the moving cable. It was no use. Instinctively they got out of the fast-moving bucket by grabbing onto the cable for dear life, then throwing their legs up over the cable as well.

Porterfield stayed in the bucket as it sped down into the dark, gaining speed by the inch. The Mahoneys figured he was a dead man. Soon they heard the loose bucket crash into another bucket over 1,000 feet below. Clinging desperately to the coarse cable with their arms and legs, the Mahoney brothers took the ride of their lives, descending almost 2,000 feet with vertical drops topping 300 feet. Youth and luck combined to save them. Although he was bleeding and bruised, Porterfield, who remained in the bucket, also miraculously survived the free fall. Bill and Posse were too embarrassed to seek medical attention for their badly scrapped hands and legs.

A few years earlier this same aerial tram "dumped a whole shift crew down the mountainside . . . The injured men were difficult to locate in the rocks and brush, but there was only one fatality" (Wright, 1974). (Courtesy of Bill Mahoney) (H. Reid photo: Courtesy of Jerry O'Rourke)

The Sheridan Incline

A few trams ran on trestles rather than towers. One of the high Sheridan trams — called the Sheridan Incline — looked more like a giant toboggan run, or the first leg of a gigantic roller coaster ride. A lower tram (right) was built to ferry timber and materials needed for the construction of the Sheridan Incline. Wooden snowsheds soon covered most of these inclines, or earthbound trams. (Telluride Historical Museum) (H. Reid photo: Courtesy of Bill Mahoney)

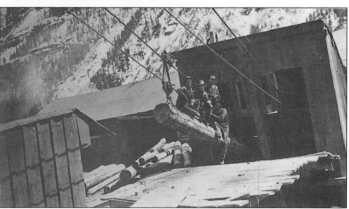

A high-country sculpture

During winter and late spring, avalanches wreaked havoc on the trams. In just seconds hurtling masses of snow smashed towers into splinters, then scattered the pieces down the mountain. To protect towers in well-known slide areas, miners built large stone structures to deflect the powerful and dangerous slides. Despite a century of winter perils, the grand apex tower on the Black Bear Mine tramway stands proudly to this day; a work of art at 12,000 feet. (Courtesy of Bill Mahoney)

More than ore and an unlikely legacy

Trams transported more than ore. They carried anything that could be heaped, jammed, or wedged into their flat-bottomed buckets. Food, nails, wood, wire, coal, sinks, heaters, bottles, boots, chairs, typewriters, and anything else needed for the operation of the high mines swayed up the cable in rusting brown buckets. Miners also came to and from work in the rhythmically bobbing buckets. Some loved to ride the tram, others abhorred it — especially in winter.

Above, several miners pose comfortably at the upper tram terminal of the Alta Mine

(possibly the Gold King Mine). The Alta tram dropped down to its mill near Ophir, where the crushed ore would be transferred to Rio Grande Southern freight cars.

No miner could have predicted, however, that the legacy of these aerial tramways would manifest itself as a vital part of one of America's most popular and expensive recreational activities: skiing. All one has to do is watch the fast-moving ultra-modern gondolas whisk skiers (and snowboarders) to some of the highest peaks and deepest bowls in the Colorado Rockies. (Courtesy of Walker Collection)

An educational landmark

The scenic view on this stereocard carries the caption: "Light and shadow playing over Ballard Mts. (S.E.), above Telluride, Colo." Telluride's new school, the large two-story brick building in the foreground still holds its place as one of Telluride's prominent landmarks. It cost $24,000 to construct in 1895.

"In 1881-82 the first public school in this present County [then Ouray County], was taught by Charles Jeffs, in the house of F. R. Hamilton, at San Miguel, with only eight or ten pupils. In 1893 the County, with an assessed valuation of $1,300,000, shows six school districts, eight schools with 235 sittings, a school population of from six to twenty-one years of age of 383 . . . with an average attendance (on account of the roving character of our people) of 160, or 42 percent, ten teachers with an average salary per month of $72, or excluding Telluride, of $62" (*Telluride and San Miguel County*, 1894). (Courtesy of Joann and Wes Leech)

A school buggy and an electrified kitchen

Some students took this "school bus" to and from the combination grade school and high school. During winter several of the students rode in a large open sleigh. Telluride's public school boasted the "world's first electrified school kitchen," thanks to Lucien Nunn's power plant. (Telluride Historical Museum)

School children

Agroup of Telluride primary school children pose with their teachers (and possibly the principal) on the front steps of the new school. A graceful stone archway highlights the entrance. (Telluride Historical Museum)

CHAPTER TWO: TELLURIDE THRIVES (1890s)

Downtown Telluride thrives

In the mid-1890s, with a bustling population topping 2,500, downtown Telluride thrived. Several new businesses blossomed along the dirt main street. This scene includes "the Cosmopolitan Saloon (beginning at far right) — at 109 East Colorado Avenue — a barber shop, saloon and gambling hall, stationary [sic] and drugstore, with a second[-]story business, run by J. F. Quine & Company [bottom image shows Fourth of July gathering in front of this store]. Charles E. Ross, Jeweler, occupied the fancy pressed-metal building, while Gents Furnishings and the H. C. Baisch [D]rugstore are in the corner building, where the Elks lodge met (upstairs). The First National Bank building stands across North Fir Street" (Collman and McCoy, 1991). Farther up the street are the New Sheridan Hotel and the San Miguel County Courthouse.

In the top photograph, men in suits standing on the boardwalk and a covered delivery wagon are partially obscured by a long mule pack train. This train appears to be the one that hauled the tram cable up Bear Creek to the Nellie Mine. A thick layer of coarse stone had been carefully spread along the center of the atypically wide Colorado Avenue. (Byers photo: Courtesy of Walker Collection) (Courtesy of Irene R. Visintin and Elvira F. Visintin Wunderlich)

CHAPTER TWO: TELLURIDE THRIVES (1890s)

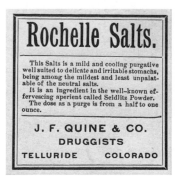

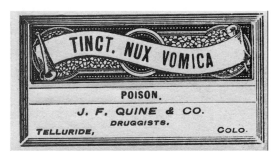

Embossed bottles and paper labels

Late 19th century drugstores frequently embossed their names on prescription bottles. Telluride's J.F. Quine and Company followed this tradition. Quine also affixed paper labels to bottles containing a wide variety of substances. (Author's photo: Courtesy of Bill Ellicott) (Courtesy of Joann and Wes Leech)

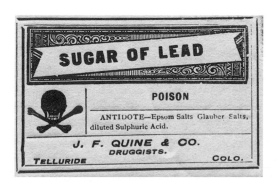

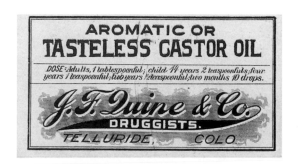

CHAPTER TWO: TELLURIDE THRIVES (1890s)

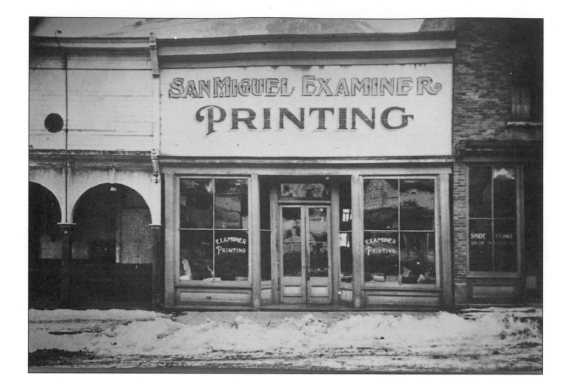

Mining camp news

Published weekly between 1897 and 1929, the *San Miguel Examiner* chronicled local happenings for the news-hungry population. Regional newspapers proved influential in remote mining camps like Telluride because they constituted the sole source of information for many of their loyal readers. Publishers of these provincial publications often slanted the news to reflect their particular political biases — a practice not unheard of today.

"No Cheap Advertising Accepted" bragged this early *Examiner* receipt. One can only surmise that "cheap advertising" referred to the less than reputable sporting activities astride East Pacific Avenue. The photograph showcases the *Examiner's* place of business on Colorado Avenue on a winter day. (Telluride Historical Museum) (Courtesy of P. David Smith)

Telluride, Colo., *Jan 1st* 189*7*

M *W. M. Randall*

TO THE SAN MIGUEL EXAMINER, DR.

WOODMANSEE & SUMNER. Publishers.

Published Weekly. Guaranteed Largest Circulation in the County. No Cheap Advertising Accepted.

Commercial Printing of all Kinds Latest Ideas in Type Designing Largest Stock in Western Colorado

SUBSCRIPTION RATES: $2.00 PER YEAR;   SIX MONTHS, $1.00.   INVARIABLY IN ADVANCE.

To adv for Dec — *$3.00*

Paid

C. A. Woodman

The oldest paper

The *Telluride Journal* with receipts like the one shown here, legitimately claimed to be the "Oldest Paper in San Miguel County." Charles F. Painter, the business manager of this daily publication, owned interests in several other Telluride enterprises. He was also the grandfather of author and historian David Lavender. (Courtesy of P. David Smith)

"Careful and competent merchant buyers"

All lines of merchandising are well represented by staunch, enterprising business houses, both wholesale and retail. There are, perhaps, more than a dozen houses that carry stock aggregating $20,000 each, and every want is abundantly provided for by careful and competent merchant buyers. Our merchants universally are enterprising and competitive, which gives to the consumer a good market in which to buy" (*Telluride and San Miguel County,* 1894).

The Sheridan (Hotel) Building, featured here, exemplified one of Telluride's staunch business houses during 1890s. It added a third story in 1899. (Reprinted from *Telluride and San Miguel County,* 1894)

The San Juan Hardware

Catering mostly to mining companies, the San Juan Hardware proprietors depended on the Rio Grande Southern to bring them their supplies. Except for the year after the silver crash in the summer of 1893, the 1890s proved to be a banner decade for selling merchandise in Telluride. (Reprinted from *Telluride and San Miguel County*, 1894)

CHAPTER TWO: TELLURIDE THRIVES (1890S)

Telluride, Colorado, May 31 1897

M H. B. Adsit

In account with

W. M. RANDALL,

Wholesale and Retail

COMMISSION MERCHANT,

Dealer in

FRUITS, PRODUCE, FRESH AND SALT MEATS, HAY AND GRAIN.

Special Prices on Large Orders.

SPECIALTIES

Butter, Ranch Eggs, Fish, Oysters, Potatoes, Onions, And all Kinds of Vegetables.

SPECIALTIES

Bananas, Oranges, Lemons, Berries, California, Utah and Colorado GREEN FRUITS Of all Kinds.

Early stores solicited the big mines

Small establishments like these competed for the mammoth mine business. A contract with the Tomboy or the Smuggler-Union, both of which employed hundreds of people, meant almost certain financial success. These receipts had no need to carry a specific street address, an indication of the small mountain town's mining camp status. (Both courtesy of P. David Smith)

Telluride, Colorado, Aug 17 1899

M

To **Miners Meat Market,** Dr.

JOHN GAULT, Proprietor.

Wholesale and Retail

Fresh and Cured Meats

RANCH PRODUCE, POULTRY, BUTTER AND EGGS . . .

Groceries for the high mines

Early photographers found mules laden with groceries (above) more fascinating than the warehouses that supplied them (below). The sign for the bank that Butch Cassidy robbed appears to the right in the street scene. Across Colorado Avenue is another early Telluride newspaper, *The Republican*, with political leanings that probably matched its name.

Among other foods, carefully packed wooden crates contained oranges, bananas, lemons, berries, peaches, eggs, fish, oysters, potatoes, butter, and onions. Tons of fresh fruit from fertile valleys near Grand Junction, Colorado, wound its way up to the mines on the backs of pack animals. The tattered paper label on this old crate (right) dates to early 1900s. (W. J. Carpenter photo: Denver Public Library, Western History Department) (Author's photo: Author's collection) (Telluride Historical Museum)

CHAPTER TWO: TELLURIDE THRIVES (1890s)

"Telluride has ten saloons and plans for a church"

In 1894 community stalwarts explained that: "The fact that any given place has a multiplicity of churches does not necessitate that it is a specially religious community; very often it is quite the opposite, and conversely the statement that Telluride has only one church does not necessarily imply that we are, for that reason, irreligious, but it does show, and that to our credit, that we are not stupidly and doggedly denominational" (*Telluride and San Miguel County*, 1894).

Why the questionable logic? Perhaps the town fathers were still smarting from a moral slap delivered by Ouray's *Solid Muldoon* in 1885: "Ouray has four churches and fourteen saloons. Telluride has ten saloons and plans for a church." Telluride's first house of worship, the Congregational Church (above), could count on about seventy-five faithful souls to occupy its pews each Sunday morning. Having a preacher behind the pulpit was another matter. In 1892 an entry in the Telluride section of the state business directory read: "Congregational Church, no pastor." (Reprinted from *Telluride and San Miguel County*, 1894)

Dispensing justice and more

Built in 1885, San Miguel County's first courthouse burned within a year. In 1887, the distinctive brick structure shown here replaced it on the other side of Colorado Avenue. Dispensing more than justice, it hosted town meetings, dances, and even church dinners. Legal matters continue to be deliberated in its historic chambers. (Reprinted from *Telluride and San Miguel County*, 1894)

See-through voting

For decades voters in San Miguel County dropped their ballots through the slot in the top of this old wood and glass ballot box. To open it required three officials, each with a different key. (Author's photos: Courtesy of Jerry O'Rourke)

CHAPTER TWO: TELLURIDE THRIVES (1890s)

A lot of silver coins slid down the slot

A lot of silver coins slid down the slot of this Mills gaming machine in the Pick and Gad. The Mills company starting producing Dewey uprights (sometimes with a music box) in 1899. It sported a likeness of Admiral Dewey, a patriot of the time. (Author's photo: Courtesy of Jerry O'Rourke)

What the miners wanted

An eyewitness wrote about miners' weekends. "What they wanted most was drink and gambling, dancing and women. And what they wanted was easily available. . . . Large combination saloon and gambling halls (some with restaurants — all with free lunch) ran twenty-four hours a day and three hundred and dixty-five [sic] days a year. . . . Equally popular and well patronized were the Silver Bell and White House dance halls; big houses called the Pick and Gad [above] and the Big Swede's; and the cribs, a series of small shacks each with one female occupant" (Belsey, 1962).

The modest brick exterior of the Pick and Gad does not betray the activities that transpired within. "Gad" is a Cornish term for a pointed iron bar used to loosen ore. "A smart and aging woman" by the name of Laura LaRue owned the Pick and Gad. This notorious "big house" still stands (above) on South Pine Street. (Author's photo)

A choice of the immoral

Along East Pacific Avenue, one block south of Colorado Avenue, miners could have their choice of the illegal and immoral. Shown here is the interior of an unidentified saloon and gambling club complete with musicians playing in the background. "The big 'houses' were the 'class' of the red light district. Here, the girls acted more lady-like but not more modest. They dressed in somewhat fashionable garb, peddled to them in the afternoons by a respected clothing establishment" (Belsey, 1962). (Denver Public Library, Western History Department)

The Silver Bell

One of the "big houses," the Silver Bell still stands (although little remains of the original structure) on the corner of Pacific Avenue and Spruce Street (above). "The original building was constructed in the 1880s and at first consisted of a two-story place called McPhersons' Rooming House, which adjoined the Silver Bell Saloon. On July 4, 1890, a disgruntled customer set fire to the Silver Bell, and the rooming house was severely damaged. Using material salvaged from the original structure, Barney Gabardi and a partner rebuilt the structure and ran it as a saloon and gambling hall" (Fetter and Fetter, 1979). (Author's photo)

Cribs

"The denizens of the cribs were older and on the way down on the down-and-out pathway. The front window of each crib was a show-window: if the blind was pulled, the store was full" (Belsey, 1962). By the time this photograph was taken of "the line," most of the cribs astride East Pacific Avenue had been moved, torn down, or like these (above) stood vacant. The few that remain along East Pacific Avenue have been tastefully restored as residential homes. In the bottom photograph the center crib in the older photograph can be seen in its restored condition. (Telluride Historical Museum) (Author's photo)

Cattle interests

Outfits like Galloway and Sons, Nelson and Field, M. W. Powell Cattle, and Anderson Brothers and Nachtrieb, among others, ran cattle on medium to large spreads from Telluride to Lone Cone Mountain. "The mode of raising cattle in this county has changed from what it was ten years ago. Instead of depending on range feed the entire year, the cattlemen have been preparing feed with which to winter their stock, thereby avoiding heavy losses during the winter months" (*Telluride and San Miguel County*, 1894). (Reprinted from *Telluride and San Miguel County*, 1894).

Dry Creek Cowboys

Telluride's Board of Trade boasted that, "The conclusion that can be clearly reached from a review of the cattle industry of the County, from an experience of ten years past, is that it has been largely profitable to those engaged in it and that there is plainly unfolded before them a future of constantly increasing prosperity" (*Telluride and San Miguel County*, 1894). These cowboys might have argued that they had yet to become prosperous on their meager wages. (Telluride Historical Museum)

"Fructifying touch"

Wilson Peak looms behind a large field of hay cut and raked by horse-drawn equipment. In the left center of the photograph a small blurry white spot is visible directly behind the top of the telephone pole. This white spot is a small area tromped bare by horses and men working an overshot stacker. Like its name indicates, an overshot stacker was a common piece of old farm equipment used to stack piles of hay. With a magnifying glass one can even see the stacker in an upright position, ready to catapult another load of hay onto the stack.

Glowing words from the city fathers asserted that the county, "still contains within its borders room and opportunity for the development of a thousand happy and contented homes. It is a section of broad mesas and beautiful valleys, whose fertile soil needs but the fructifying touch of the waters of the living mountain streams to become fruitful producers of all the cereal, vegetable or horticultural products known in the temperate zone" (*Telluride and San Miguel County*, 1894). (Fort Lewis College, Center of Southwest Studies)

A Telluride wedding

This is an 1898 wedding photograph of Edith M. Cramer and Barge Hiskey. Their daughter, Dorothy Hiskey Evans, who now resides in Grand Junction, Colorado, still has this time-worn image taken by the Moore Brothers studio over a century ago (left). Dorothy recalls that her father told of "strapping on long wooden skis" to inspect power lines and poles for avalanche damage. This suggests that her father worked for Lucien Nunn's power company. The Hiskey's ornate wedding certificate (below) is still treasured by their daughter. (Moore Brothers photo: Courtesy of Dorothy H. Evans) (Author's photo: Courtesy of Dorothy H. Evans)

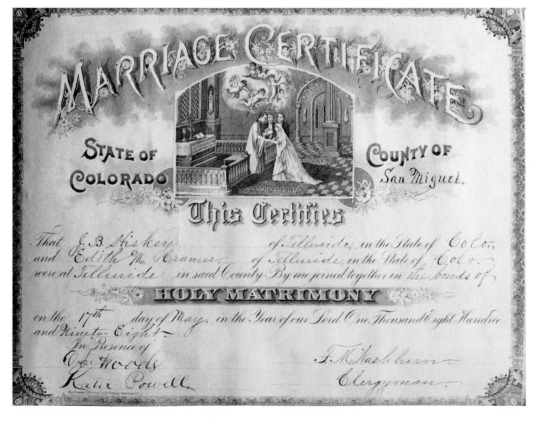

Courtney

TELLURIDE
COLORADO

A pin for the ages

The Courtney Studio of
Telluride took this early
photograph (left) of Edith Hiskey
(left), Barge Hiskey, and a friend,
Miss Agnes Warner. Notice the
pin on the collar of Edith Hiskey's
dress. Her daughter, Dorothy
Hiskey Evans, still prizes this
delicate sword-shaped pin
featuring inlaid garnets (below).
(Courtney photo: Courtesy of
Dorothy H. Evans) (Author's
photo: Courtesy of Dorothy
H. Evans)

CHAPTER TWO: TELLURIDE THRIVES (1890s)

CHAPTER TWO: TELLURIDE THRIVES (1890s)

Into a new century

Fierce winter storms often buried Colorado Avenue under several feet of snow. Left, even a man in his wagon with sleigh runners is stuck. But no one, including the fellow with the shovel and several people along the boardwalks, seems eager to assist.

This image also constitutes a visual metaphor for things to come in the remote mountain mining town of Telluride. Soon to be stuck in labor and financial strife, Telluride seemed neither able nor willing to extricate itself from its problems. (Courtesy of Dorothy H. Evans)

CHAPTER THREE
TURBULENCE IN

Martin G. Wenger recalled that on the advent of the new century, his brother and father "had secured some short pieces of three inch pipe and had loaded them with sticks of dynamite. They took these to a field about a block from town in preparation of setting off the loud blasts as part of . . . an experience that only one generation of people would live to see . . . the 'Turn of the Century.'" Wenger described what he witnessed as a young boy: "At midnight, pandemonium broke loose. Blasts of dynamite on the mountain sides, shootings of pistols, the church bells and the old fire department bells were rung and the mill whistles were blown for about an hour. It impressed me very much."

Telluride's boisterous 20th-century start set the tenor for its first decade. Mine owners and prosperous businessmen walked the wooden sidewalks in fine clothes, smoked expensive cigars, danced the night away at gala balls in Denver, and vacationed in Europe. Most underground miners, however, earned less than the expected $3.00 for a ten or twelve-hour day of backbreaking labor. "Outside" or "surface laborers" were lucky to earn $2.50 for a ten-hour day, while mill workers brought home $4.00 for a twelve-hour day. There were few, if any, benefits. And most miners paid for room and board, so

they ended up in debt to the company. When the owners introduced the fathom system (meaning wages were based on the number of six-foot cubes of ore a miner could mine in a day), the Smuggler-Union men had had enough. They wanted nothing to do with this fathom system, the equivalent of factory piecework but with bodies of ore. The miners went on strike in early May of 1901.

In a pattern that was to become familiar in several San Juan mines over the next few years, the owners brought in nonunion replacement workers (derisively dubbed "scabs" by the unions). Friction immediately mounted between striking union men and scabs. In this tense atmosphere in November of 1901 a load of hay mysteriously caught fire at the mouth of the Smuggler-Union. The billowing smoke and intense heat was quickly sucked deep into the mine, while on the surface the fire spread rapidly. The sequence of events that followed remains controversial, but no one can dispute that the Smuggler-Union tunnel was ruined, the boardinghouse burned to the ground, and twenty-eight men died. An eye-witness reported that the funeral procession "was the longest in the history of Telluride." That same year a Pandora Mill fire claimed — some say — twenty lives, several men were shot during labor

PARADISE (1900s)

disputes, and deadly plots were hatched by miners and mine owners alike. Eventually the state militia arrived to quell the violence, although some believe they added to it.

As if this were not enough, nature decided to create even more havoc. On February 28, 1902, a massive snowslide came roaring down Cornet Creek, taking the Liberty Bell's boardinghouse and some bunkhouses with it. While rescue teams frantically searched for victims, another slide ran, killing two of the rescuers. Then a third slide let go nearby, sweeping more men to their deaths. By the end of the day sixteen men were dead and ten injured. Some bodies were not recovered until spring. That summer lightning struck the Liberty Bell's ore-cart rails, electrocuting three workers in the bowels of the mine. To this grisly total was added the scores of lives taken by accidental explosions, miner's "consumption," mercury poisoning, cave-ins, and everyday accidents.

Even during these turbulent times, a young bride of a Tomboy miner still found adventure and joy in the high country. She poignantly described the vicissitudes of her life — as witnessed in the excerpts that follow — from her classic work, *Tomboy Bride*. Down in Telluride politics still attracted considerable attention. Presidential candidates like socialist Eugene Debs and free-silver advocate William Jennings Bryan rode the rails to the remote mining town to deliver fiery speeches pregnant with promises. Audience members fresh from their favorite saloons often cheered or jeered, depending on the general mood of the crowd.

As the first decade of the new century drew to a close, the sounds of the great Pandora Mill's stamps — the heartbeat of Telluride — remained strong. By 1909 the Telluride district had produced over $60,000,000 in mineral-rich ore. Over $13,000,000 of that amount came from the Liberty Bell, Smuggler-Union, and Tomboy between 1905 and 1911. As a by-product of this success, prosperity prevailed for most townspeople despite all the mining troubles and natural disasters. That the decade ended with one more natural disaster hardly seemed inappropriate. The Trout Lake damn burst, sending torrents of water careening over the San Miguel River banks. Near Ames, the rushing wall of water nearly wiped out Lucien Nunn's alternating-current power plant. Even worse, miles of railroad track between Ames and Placerville were destroyed, isolating Telluride for some time.

The eye of the beholder

While surveying this scene, historians painstakingly point out the location of the old schoolhouse, San Miguel County Courthouse, New Sheridan Hotel, Congregational Church, Town Hall, First National Bank steeples, Finn Hall, and the Rio Grande Southern Railroad depot (foreground). More aesthetically inclined viewers see it differently: "To those desiring to climb the most rugged mountains, visit wild, dismal and almost impenetrable canons, and 'drink in' the grandest of all American scenery, and all within a days ramble from a comfortable hotel, we should certainly recommend a visit to Telluride" (printed on a receipt from The Cash Grocery, 1894). (J. Byers photo: American Heritage Center, University of Wyoming)

"This is Great — finest-ever"

Written a thousand different ways, praises for Telluride's mountain paradise spread throughout America on popular turn-of-the-century picture postcards. For over a century writers have tried to capture the majesty of this setting. But mere words never do justice to such indescribable grandeur. Mount Wilson (not to be confused with nearby Wilson Peak) constituted one of the most favored postcard scenes (above). (Postcard: Courtesy of P. David Smith)

CHAPTER THREE: TURBULENCE IN PARADISE (1900s)

Frozen splendor

In 1908, Telluride photographer Joseph Byers (successor to Moore Brothers photography) recorded this classic winter image of Bridal Veil Falls and powerhouse (a small hydroelectric plant). Built in 1907, the powerhouse generated electricity for Pandora far below. An aerial tramway ferried people and supplies between Pandora and the powerhouse. Those who rode this tramway surely never tired of the sublime views.

"Bridal Veil Falls . . . set like a continually changing gem against a stern and forbidding cliff, its perpendicular fall of 380 feet commands the admiration of all. Were it in Switzerland, its beauties would be commented upon by poem and painting, and thousands would cross the sea to gaze upon its matchless beauty" (printed on a receipt from The Cash Grocery, 1894). (J. Byers photo: Courtesy of Martin A. Wenger)

"It swarms with the fish"

"Trout Lake [originally called San Miguel Lake], but a few miles from Telluride is one of the largest and most beautiful of the many lakes in the state. It swarms with the fish that gives its name, and is destined to become a noted and popular resort" (printed on a receipt from The Cash Grocery, 1894). Images of the surrounding mountains reflect off of the calm waters, doubling their beauty.

For those who preferred hunting: "In by far the largest part of the County an abundance of game affords the sportsman ample exercise for his skill. Deer and grouse are plentiful in the foothills and mesas, while in the more mountainous section black and cinnamon bear and the mountain lion can yet be found in large numbers" (printed on a receipt from The Cash Grocery, 1894). (Courtesy of Walker Collection)

Marriage in the mountains

A wedding party poses near the water tower at the Trout Lake station. Trout Lake's alpine splendor served as the setting for several weddings in the early 1900s. One might surmise that Trout Lake is as close as possible to a marriage made in heaven. (Telluride Historical Museum)

CHAPTER THREE: TURBULENCE IN PARADISE (1900S)

Horses, wagons, and buggies for rent

Customers line the street in front of Herbert Feed and Sale Stable on Pine Street. "Human transportation to and from mines was by saddle horses from three big livery stables; cost per one-way trip, $2.00. These horses were trained to return down the mountain to their stable, without a rider, after the miner had completed his trip. It was a common sight to see strings of saddle horses being led to the mines on pay-day" (Belsey, 1962). These people do not appear to be miners, although they may be headed for one of the high mines. Two dogs nonchalantly watch the proceedings. In 1907 Telluride dog licenses (below) cost two dollars and fifty cents. (Telluride Historical Museum) (Author's photo: Courtesy of Ralph Kemper)

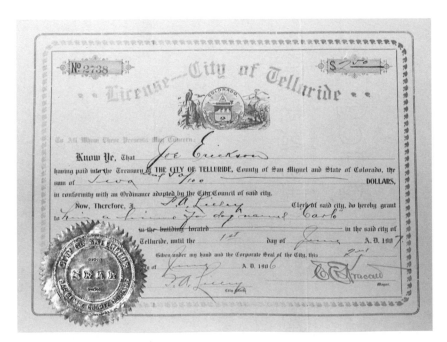

CHAPTER THREE: TURBULENCE IN PARADISE (1900s)

"Our Trip to the Tomboy and the Top of the Range"

On August 11, 1907, Esther Tallman wrote an account of her trip to the high country. "About 9 a.m., three saddle horses were brought to our gate, for which Anna and I, dressed in divided skirts, and Charles, were waiting."

"We mounted and after riding through town, took the famous road leading to the Smuggler and Tomboy Mines. This road took several years to build and cost $40,000. While it is a fine road and kept in thorough repair, it is dangerous on account of there being so much travel on it. The road is in constant use by the six-horse ore wagons coming from the mines to Telluride and back, the numerous pack-trains,

many men going to and from the mines, tourists and visitors. Only last week there was a frightful runaway in which the buggy dashed down the road and met a mule pack-train. The driver could not get the mules out of the way, and as there was not room for both the horses shied, dashed over the side of the mountain and rolled to the bottom. Thus one can see that it is much safer to make the trip on horseback." The women pictured here in downtown Telluride may well have had a similar experience. (Reprinted from a letter written by Mrs. Esther Tallman, August 11, 1907: Courtesy of Dr. James Parker.) (Courtesy of P. David Smith)

CHAPTER THREE: TURBULENCE IN PARADISE (1900s)

Burros of the band

Telluride Shoeing and Carriage Shop may well have supplied some of the shoes for the burros of the band. (Telluride Historical Museum) (Courtesy of P. David Smith)

Blacksmith shop

Blacksmith business was big business in the early 1900s. Shown here in his shop is John Keith. An able blacksmith could earn a comfortable living. Large mines had their own state-of-the-art blacksmith facilities. The Telluride Hardware Co. sold blacksmith supplies opposite the post office. (Telluride Historical Museum) (Courtesy of Ralph Kemper)

The heartbeat of Telluride

Twenty-four hours a day the constant, dull pounding from the Smuggler-Union mills in Pandora (above) could be heard throughout downtown Telluride. Up close the din was deafening. In 1907 Esther Tallman wrote: "We went through the mills where there were sixty stamps working at once and so much noise! Why you could not even hear your own voice! I don't understand the stamps well enough to describe them better, but I do know they were noisy!" After the old mill and cyanide plant burned in 1920, the Gray Mill that replaced it had no stamps to pound. (Courtesy of Walker Collection)

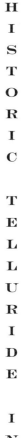

Working the dirt

Agroup of miners and a small boy pose by a water flume and a crude sluice. They appear to be working the dirt at a fairly low elevation. Precious little information remains about the hundreds of men who worked small claims scattered throughout the San Juan Mining District. (Courtesy of Walker Collection)

CHAPTER THREE: TURBULENCE IN PARADISE (1900s)

Too many funerals

Most miners worked ten to twelve-hour shifts, seven days a week, in appalling conditions. "They were paid $3.00 per day (some, but not many, got more), and they paid $1.00 per day for board and bunk. By modern standards, by any standards, they led a bleak and dangerous life. . . . A few, very few, had families living in town. Welshmen, Irish, Finlanders, Swedes, Italians and Greeks. Predominantly foreigners" (Belsey, 1962).

"Death was common at the mines and often grisly. At those altitudes pneumonia was nearly one hundred percent fatal for those who contracted it. Men fell down shafts, loose boulders sometimes caved in on them from stope roofs. A driller might set off, in his own face, dynamite that had failed to explode when the preceding shift had fired its rounds. . . . But seldom were disasters as horrifying as the Smuggler-Union fire on November 20, 1901 [28 men died] and the Liberty Bell avalanches of February 28, 1902 [16 men died]" (Lavender, 1987). "At the Alta [Mine], mercury poisoning, resulting in loss of teeth or even death, was a turn-of-the-century hazard that fueled the crises at the mines" (Fetter and Fetter, 1979).

Although they lacked formal education, miners had little trouble comprehending that their dangerous daily drudgery enriched only the already-wealthy mine owners. As years passed, resentment among the miners intensified. Finally, these abominable conditions led a group of Telluride miners to join the militant Western Federation of Miners on July 28, 1896. It was time to share the wealth. (Courtesy of Prisilla Robin from the Louis and Florence Adreatta collection)

Turbulence in paradise

As a young boy, Martin G. Wenger witnessed the labor strife. He recalled: "Very significant labor troubles occurred in the early 1900s. . . . They reached such proportions that before it was over the State Militia was called in to maintain peace and order.

"The first strike was called in May 1901 and was followed by much bickering on the part of both the company and the union. Nothing really was accomplished and the Smuggler resumed operations in June. By July 1, a William Barney, a non-union supporter and shift boss had disappeared. The union was suspected by many of the Telluride inhabitants to have done away with him. On the 3rd about 250 well-armed union miners surrounded the building and workings of the Smuggler-Union Mine. When the non-union miners came to work firing broke out and the non-

union men fired back and retreated to the Bullion Tunnel." Three men died and six were wounded. "The non-union men surrendered their arms on the condition they would not be molested or harmed. That afternoon the Union men lined up the non-union miners, beat some and took their shoes. They marched them over Imogene Pass to Ouray, telling them never to come back." Almost immediately, Wenger remembered, "other mines went out on strike." By July 4 an agreement, the equivalent of a modified treaty, had been reached. But neither side was satisfied.

Dashing Bulkeley Wells (second from right), shown here with a group of National Guard officers, championed the mine owners' cause in Telluride and Cripple Creek. (American Heritage Center, University of Wyoming) (Quotes from Wenger, 1978)

CHAPTER THREE: TURBULENCE IN PARADISE (1900s)

Fort Peabody

The next few years produced sporadic outbreaks of violence between miners and mine owners. The union directed much of its venom toward Arthur Collins, manager of the Smuggler, who instituted the hated contract, or fathom, system. Wenger (1978) explains: "Contract mining involved the letting of private contracts to miners, individuals or groups who were paid according to the amount of work done, instead of regular wages. These contractors had to purchase all of their supplies from the mining company and could work as many hours as they wished. The Union disagreed with this system because they said the prices paid on the contracts were lowered when soft ground was encountered but not increased when harder rock was struck." The union men also loathed purchasing equipment and supplies at inflated prices from the company.

By 1903 Telluride found itself faced with a larger and more violent strike. The miners' union demanded, among other things, $4.50 for an eight-hour day. The owners patently rejected such "absurd" demands, and hired "scabs" to replace the striking men. Tempers flared. Soon bloody fighting threatened anarchy. By order of Colorado's Governor James H. Peabody, who strongly favored the mine owners, hundreds of state militia (also known as the National Guard) arrived in Telluride to protect the strike breakers. To ward off more bloodshed, union trouble makers were herded into a makeshift metal stockade on Colorado Avenue, then ignominiously shipped out on the Rio Grande Southern.

In a futile attempt to prevent these same "union trouble makers" from sneaking back into Telluride, the militiamen stationed themselves in a small, hastily constructed, shelter on top of Imogene Pass, over 13,100 feet above sea level. Union workers facetiously dubbed this grayish rock shelter "Fort Peabody." (Telluride Historical Museum)

Men in uniform

At first glance, one does not notice (right) two of Governor Peabody's uniformed National Guardsmen with their rifles. Yet they stand erect on the boardwalk in front of the F. D. Work and Co. store at the corner of Colorado Avenue and South Alder. Even the shopkeeper wearing the white apron is armed with a pistol. A description with this photograph reads, "Local citizens and mine owners requested Colorado National Guard to control streets from September 1, 1903 to November 29, 1904, during strikes by the Western Federation of Miners and United Mine Workers of America."

Before the troops arrived in September of 1903 a vigilante group, the "Citizens Alliance," had taken the law into its own hands. "Quite secretly, at the height of the inflammatory incidents, the men of the town used the cover of

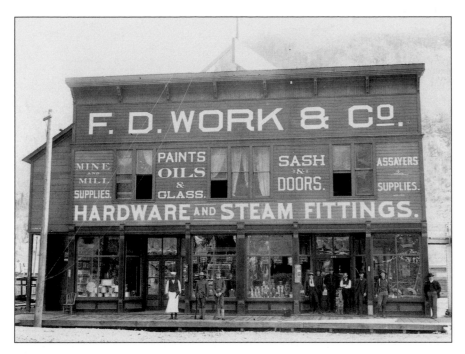

night to gather up known [union] agitators and sympathizers including a few merchants: The Citizens Alliance marched this group, maybe sixty of them, to the railroad station and deported them on a special train to the nearest town some fifty miles away" (Belsey, 1962). (J. Byers photo: Denver Public Library, Western History Department)

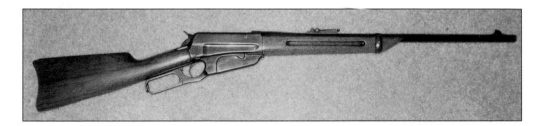

Winchester Model 95 (30 - 40 Kraig)

The National Guardsman standing on the boardwalk probably held a rifle similar to the one shown above. Although this Winchester was not standard issue (Kraig-Jorgensons of the same caliber were), it had "National Guard of Colorado" stamped in its breech and served its purpose in quelling the violence. "In those days every citizen, including the preacher, had a Colt and a Winchester" (Belsey, 1964). "Both the local residents of Telluride and visitors had to have military passes

even to appear on the town streets. And anyone was subject to arrest and deportation from the district with hardly any provocation. A resident's house could be searched at any hour of the day or night on nothing more than mere suspicion, or because the owner was thought to be harboring a striking miner or that it might contain a pistol or rifle. More than one Telluride home was left a complete shambles by unruly troopers" (Collman and McCoy, 1991). (Author's photos: Courtesy of Robert Sowada)

"Bulkeley Wells greatly impressed me when I was a youngster"

Born in Chicago, Bulkeley Wells graduated from Harvard as a mining engineer. In 1894, after taking Boston society by storm, the debonair Wells married the elegant Grace Livermore, daughter of millionaire Colonel Thomas Livermore, whose company owned the Smuggler.

Soon after their marriage Wells and his bride arrived in Colorado. There he divided his time between Telluride and the even more rarified social atmosphere of Denver. Women found the clever and strikingly handsome Wells irresistible. Indeed, prominent Denver socialite Mrs. Crawford Hill, "kept a full-length painting of him on the stair landing in her mansion."

Bulkeley Wells took over as manager of the Smuggler in 1902, after Arthur Collins was brutally assassinated by a shotgun blast while sitting in his home in Pandora. Wells unabashedly championed the owners and business interests. Soon he became a captain in the Colorado National Guard, posing as though a Greek god in the portrait shown here.

Martin G. Wenger wrote: "Bulkeley Wells greatly impressed me when I was a youngster. I often saw him about town. He had a military bearing and was also always dressed immaculately in everyday clothes and when we were attending functions." (American Heritage Center, University of Wyoming)

A victory parade

Ultimately the influence and money of the mine owners, combined with the power of an arch-conservative governor, prevailed. By 1905 strikes in mining towns across Colorado, including Telluride, were broken. Miners went back to work for the same low wages, in the same appalling conditions.

Here proud troopers of the Colorado National Guard celebrate their victory over the miners during a parade in downtown Denver. (American Heritage Center, University of Wyoming)

For those who quelled the violence

Active service badges were awarded to the members of the militia who served in Colorado City, Cripple Creek, Telluride, and Trinidad. Appropriately, Governor Peabody's visage appears on the medallion. (M. S. Strain photo: Courtesy of Robert Sowada)

CHAPTER THREE: TURBULENCE IN PARADISE (1900s)

An elegant society wedding

In June, 1906, Robert Livermore Jr., brother-in-law to Bulkeley Wells, married Gwendolen Young at "Glen Eyrie," at the Colorado Springs estate of railroad magnate General William Jackson Palmer. Grace Wells stands to the left of the groom. Bulkeley Wells stands to the right of the bride. On Bulkeley's right is Halstead Lindsley, later a prominent figure in Canadian mining together with his brother, Thayer Lindsley. With a rich father-in-law, a Harvard education, and numerous powerful connections in the mining community, Bulkeley Wells's future seemed bright. (American Heritage Center, University of Wyoming)

In the company of governors

Bulkeley Wells (standing), now an Adjutant General in the Colorado National Guard, rides in a carriage with Governor Henry A. Buchtel after his inauguration in 1907. Immediate past Governor Jesse Fuller MacDonald from Leadville, with his trademark mustache, sits next to Governor Buchtel. The General of the Colorado National Guard also rides in the ornate carriage. High-living Wells proudly wears the Peabody medal on his chest. (American Heritage Center, University of Wyoming)

Divorce and suicide

From the porch of her husband's office, Grace Livermore Wells looks into the camera. The mighty Smuggler-Union complex looms in the background. But not all was well. Although she loved Wells, she finally had enough of his long absences and well-known philandering. She divorced him in 1918. Immediately, Robert Livermore Jr. replaced Wells as manager of the Smuggler. After the divorce Bulkeley's fortunes plummeted along with the rest of the mining industry. In 1928 even the Smuggler-Union closed.

Desperately trying to regain his success and wealth, Wells made several ill-advised investments, including a disastrous radium scheme on the Colorado-Utah border. "Along the way he married a devoted and gorgeous platinum blonde. At that, Mrs. Crawford Hill reportedly took down his picture from her stair landing" (Lavender, 1987), not to mention undermining him financially.

In the early 1900s no one in Telluride would have predicted that this dashing, energetic man would eventually take his own life, rendered

unbearable by bad debt and crushed pride. Yet that is what transpired in 1931 when Bulkeley Wells put a gun to his head and pulled the trigger. He was fifty-nine. (American Heritage Center, University of Wyoming)

CHAPTER THREE: TURBULENCE IN PARADISE (1900S)

HISTORIC TELLURIDE IN RARE PHOTOGRAPHS

R. L. L. Williams   Camp Bird

Utilitarian and fun

In happier and more prosperous times, Robert Livermore Jr. poses on lengthy wooden skis with a friend near Camp Bird (on the Ouray side of Imogene Pass). Simple leather loops held the front of their boots on the skis. (American Heritage Center, University of Wyoming)

Bostonians and bullion

The Livermore family also held several mine leases in Nevada. In 1911, Robert Livermore and a friend pause by their exotic automobile "en route from Goldfield to French Mine, Nevada." They wanted to take a first-hand look at some of Livermore's leases in the Nevada gold fields.

Between 1892 and 1917 Robert Livermore kept a journal that has since been edited into a book, *Bostonians and Bullion* (Gressley, 1968). More than a history of mining during extreme labor crises, it documents a rich man's personal sojourn through America's waning mining frontier. (American Heritage Center, University of Wyoming)

National Club

In a surge of moral righteousness some Telluride citizens tried to have gambling and liquor banned in 1900. They failed. For two decades the seamy side had thrived along East Pacific Avenue (one block south of Colorado Avenue), and it would continue to do so for another two decades. The National Club on Colorado Avenue catered to thirsty customers after the turn of the century. Later it housed the Golden Rule Dry Goods Store. (Telluride Historical Museum)

Glass ad

Early bars ordered whiskey bottles embossed with their names. That way customers were reminded to refill them at the same establishment. The National Club flask shown here is a shining example of a glass ad. (Author's photo: Courtesy of Bill Ellicott)

CHAPTER THREE: TURBULENCE IN PARADISE (1900s)

"Good for 12 1/2C in Trade"

The National Club also used tokens backed with mirrors as advertisements and to make change for drink orders. Prices were generally fifteen cents for a drink, or two for a quarter. If customers paid with a quarter, they would receive this token, which was good for the other "two-for" as change. The Corner Saloon in downtown Telluride distributed metal tokens in the early 1900s. (Author's photo: Courtesy of Ralph Kemper) (Author's photo: Courtesy of Bill Ellicott)

Cosmopolitan Saloon

Well-dressed men try their luck under the watchful eye of Marshal Kenneth Angus Maclean (above), who leans his back against the ornate Cosmopolitan bar. The roulette table in the front left corner of the photograph corroborates one eyewitness's account of turn-of-the-century gambling in Telluride. "Gambling was roulette, faro bank and stud. No crap tables then. There were a few slot machines, very different than today's one-arm bandits. On those machines, the player could choose to bet even, five-to-one, ten-to-one, or twenty-to-one. No jackpots; and I think only 5c machines. It is only a guess, but I am of the opinion that the gambling 'take' was greater from the prosperous townsmen than from the 'run-of-mine' miners. Merchants, lawyers, mine officials and the gamblers and saloon owners themselves were consistent players" (Belsey, 1962). (J. Byers photo: Telluride Historical Museum)

The innocents of advertising

The Cosmopolitan Saloon, like most other saloons in Telluride, distributed its own calendars. Saloon calendars (above) frequently featured chaste female innocents — in contrast to the activities that occurred within such establishments.

Professional gamblers often took advantage of innocent, and not so innocent, adult males. "The addicts [gamblers] were ever present, the games always open and the sharpers [professionals] ever ready to make a kill. A prosperous druggist was a frequent victim; a respected banker used the wrong funds and spent time in the penitentiary and, after years, was a faro dealer; a public official was ruined; and a lodge treasurer didn't distinguish between his own funds and the lodge funds" (Belsey, 1962.). (Author's photo: Courtesy of Joann and Wes Leech)

A higher class of entertainment and a deadly legacy

A group of traveling variety-theatre performers raise a toast for the photographer. Before radio, television, and VCR movies these traveling companies enjoyed considerable fame and some fortune. Telluride citizens turned out to cheer or jeer actors in the melodrama at the Brunswick Saloon Variety Theatre on the corner of South Spruce Street and East Colorado Avenue. Coloradans will notice the porcelain "Coors Golden Beer" sign. Just down the street past the "Pabst Milwaukee Bottling Works" is the red light district.

In 1895 as Marshall Jim Clark stepped out of the Brunswick Saloon a bullet ripped into his chest. He staggered across the street to one of the cribs and died. Not many townspeople mourned his death. In fact, the city council had asked him to resign. He refused. Some say the council itself hired the gunman who fired the deadly shot from the top of the San Juan Saloon. No one will ever know, because they never caught the gunman. (Denver Public Library, Western History Department)

A selection of beer and the ice to cool it

The actors on page 151, with the exception of the small girl, hoist glasses of foaming beer. Telluride offered beer connoisseurs several choices. Three of the most popular were Coors, Pabst, and Telluride Beer (a more recent label is shown on the left). Local beer usually came by the barrel from the Telluride Brewery located in the foothills east of Telluride. Ice blocks for the ice chests used to cool the beer came from Tom McMahon's ice ponds (below) east of town. Two young men stand on log skids used during the winter to slide freshly cut ice blocks into the large storage house. (Author's photo: Courtesy of Art Pickrell) (Courtesy of Bill Mahoney)

A healthier brew

For those who preferred milk, Pilcher Dairy would deliver it to their doorsteps. In the early 1900s Kelly McKnight purchased the dairy, but kept the Pilcher name. (Photos courtesy of Bill Mahoney)

CHAPTER THREE: TURBULENCE IN PARADISE (1900S)

The New Colorado House

Located across from the Miner's Union Hospital at North Pine Street and Columbia Avenue, the New Colorado House served as a popular boarding place for travelers and actors alike. Here the same theatrical troupe (see page 151) poses for another photograph. A "Meals by Week or Day" sign hangs above the actors, while a curtain flutters out a second story window. A stove pipe lays in disrepair on the roof. This false-front hotel was later renamed the Iowa House. (Denver Public Library, Western History Department)

Posters galore

The man holding the pipe in one hand and the snowshoe in the other is not identified on the stereocard (above). His stunning collage of posters featuring actors suggests that he was an agent, ardent fan, or a theatre owner. There is a cat or rabbit with its back legs tied together on his bed. One source attributes these intriguing images to Ouray, the other to Telluride. Some of the actors on the posters probably performed in both Ouray and Telluride. (Both photos from Museum of Western Colorado)

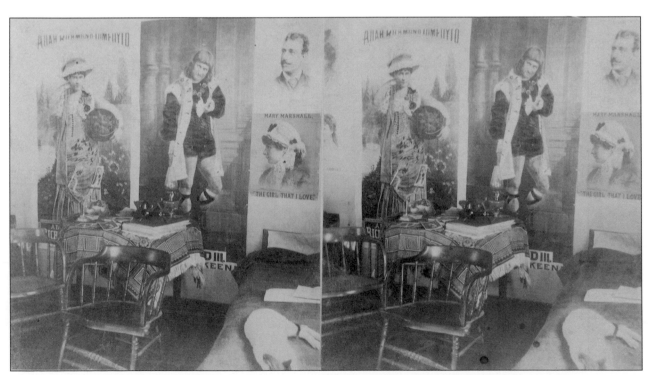

CHAPTER THREE: TURBULENCE IN PARADISE (1900s)

More than a lumber warehouse

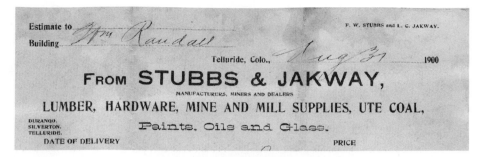

In the 1890s and early 1900s traveling thespian companies performed in the large loft above Stubbs and Jakway's lumber warehouse on East Colorado Avenue. As a young girl, longtime Telluride resident Alta Cassietto recalls seeing circus acts in the loft as well. As children, she and her friends loved to watch the circus animals parade up the long wooden ramp to Stubbs and Jakway's loft. (Courtesy of P. David Smith)

Interior of the Sheridan Opera House

Constructed in 1914, the 200-seat Sheridan Opera House supplanted Stubbs and Jakway's loft. "The theater's second-floor auditorium, which may never have served up a real opera, was small but contained the standard appurtenances — box seats, a proscenium ring with electric lights, a pointed, roll-up curtain. It also had seats that could be slid under the stage to make room for formal dances — men in white ties, women in long white gloves and long skirts billowing over a multitude of petticoats" (Lavender, 1987). (Telluride Historical Museum)

Sophisticated ladies

Sophisticated young Telluride ladies like this one probably participated in many opening nights at the Opera House. (American Heritage Center, University of Wyoming)

CHAPTER THREE: TURBULENCE IN PARADISE (1900S)

The Davis home

This sturdy brick home on the northwest corner at North Oak Street and Columbia Avenue served as a hospital during the 1918 flu epidemic. Mining and real estate entrepreneur E. L. Davis (inset) lived here. "It is sometimes called the Wagner house, after a woman who [supposedly] cleaned the attic and basement. She later moved to a hotel in Arizona to have valets and butlers" (Fetter and Fetter, 1979). (Reprinted from *Telluride and San Miguel County,* 1894) (Author's photo)

Judges' homes

Telluride judges lived in these classic turn-of-the-century homes. Judge Herbert Dill and his family occupied a dignified brick home (above) on Aspen Street. Judge Everett Vernon's family resided in an attractive wooden domicile on North Oak Street. (Photos courtesy of Bill Mahoney)

CHAPTER THREE: TURBULENCE IN PARADISE (1900S)

The Wunderlich home

Mr. and Mrs. Oscar Wunderlich sit on the front porch of their home on the southwest corner of Colorado Avenue and Townsend Street. Their horse is hitched to the buggy by the fence. A crude but serviceable plank walkway passes in front of their home. (Courtesy of Irene R. Visintin and Elvira F. Visintin Wunderlich)

Cozy interiors

Many Telluride homes had cozy, well-lit interiors. A Telluride pennant hangs over this living room with its striking oriental rug and grand piano. (Courtesy of Bill Mahoney)

Heading for a company home in the high country

In 1903 Mathew Thomas and his bride prepare to move their belongings to the Tomboy Mine, high in Savage Basin. One pack horse carries a large trunk, box springs and full sacks, the other a rolled mattress, metal bed frame and suitcase. The Thomases undoubtedly knew that their company home would be a spartan one.

Behind them is Telluride City Hall at the corner of North Fir Street and West Columbia Avenue with its sign: "Police Court, Justice of the Peace." The original Charles F. Painter home can be seen tucked among the trees in the center of the photograph. (American Heritage Center, University of Wyoming)

CHAPTER THREE: TURBULENCE IN PARADISE (1900s)

"A fearful and continuous menace"

Timed hose-cart races like the one pictured here (right), with the towers of the San Miguel Courthouse and First National Bank Building in the background, were taken seriously. "Fire, as it was in the Comstock camp and most western boom towns, was a fearful and continuous menace to Telluride. It was every able-bodied man's obligation and privilege to man the hose-carts when, day or night, a roar of pistol shots and a clanging fire bell sounded alarm . . . The Firemen were amateurs, the fire-fighting equipment primitive, but Telluride had one big asset in fighting fire. The town had an enormous supply of the purest, Sparkletts-tasting, water impounded in a big reservoir on the high mountain to the north . . . when a fire hose was turned on, it took four strong men to hold the nozzle and direct the stream of water — it would tear through the walls of any building" (Belsey, 1962).

Penciled on the back of one archival copy of the full-view photograph (right) is: "Colorado, Telluride, snow was brought down from mountains for eastern guest entertainment, 6 ft of snow fell that day in Telluride, July 4, 1909." It turns out that the date and perhaps the rest of the information written on this photograph are incorrect, as explained in the next caption. (Courtesy of P. David Smith and Dorothy H. Evans) (Inset courtesy of Bill Mahoney)

Leader of the team

On the back of another early copy of the full-view photograph (above), Dorothy H. Evans's mother, Edith Cramer Hiskey, wrote: "Agnes Warner and myself were there on that hose race [day], [in] Telluride, Colorado. Barge leads the team. Brother Charley Cramer pulls the hose from the hydrant. July 4, 1896." This date is thirteen years earlier than the date given on the archival copy of photograph. Further support for the earlier date comes from the "Spencer Wallpaper" business (notice the small sign in the photograph on the opposite page). Spencer sold wallpaper for only two years, 1896 and 1897. In the right image a maturer Barge Hiskey poses proudly with the hose cart he helped race along Colorado Avenue in 1896. (Courtesy of Dorothy H. Evans)

Trails to the high mines

In the San Juans, the high mines ruled. Telluride owed its very existence to them. Since trails to the high mines served as their lifelines, it is no surprise that trails received considerable attention. Right, the new and improved Marshall Tunnel (also called the Social Tunnel) is featured on an old postcard. A man and his horse look back through the tunnel at the photographer. For years pack trains and people funneled through the Social Tunnel during every daylight hour. (Postcard: Author's collection)

Hauling the timber

Imagine the effort it took to haul this sizable piece of lumber from Telluride to the Tomboy. Then consider the thousands of pieces of timber that helped crib the Tomboy Mine, construct the buildings, and stabilize the trail. An unknown photographer recorded this view of a six-horse team on its way to the Tomboy. (Courtesy of Walker Collection)

A section of Tomboy road

An early stereocard offers a dramatic perspective of the precipitous character of the Tomboy "road." Small wonder that men and animals arrived exhausted after trudging for over four miles up a trail that gained over 3,000 vertical feet from Telluride to the Tomboy. From a distance the driver of this freight wagon looks at the photographer. Safely descending steep mine trails often demanded more diligence and work than ascending them. Hauling anything up or down this road during winter was extremely treacherous, yet the heavy traffic remained almost constant throughout the year. (Denver Public Library, Western History Department)

A premier packer

Considered one of the best packers in the San Juans, Alex Carriere is shown with a long string of mules at the Bullion Tunnel, part of the Smuggler-Union mining complex. It is difficult to exaggerate how dangerous these trails became during winter. (Courtesy of Bill Mahoney)

CHAPTER THREE: TURBULENCE IN PARADISE (1900s)

"Quite a little town"

In 1907 Esther Tallman (see page 133) arrived at the Tomboy at 11,465 feet in altitude. Later she wrote: "There are about three hundred men at the mines and mill, many of whom have their families, so there is quite a little town around the Tom Boy." Here this small city in the sky spreads out in the thin air of Savage Basin. A school, post office, gymnasium, boardinghouses, company houses, stores, and even tennis courts comprised the impressive Tomboy. Yet, what one cannot see — the seemingly endless labyrinth of shafts and tunnels — was even more impressive. Millions of dollars in gold ore came from the extensive workings in Savage Basin that encompassed other mining properties such as the Japan Mine and Argentine Mine. (Telluride Historical Museum)

Tomboy employees

Hundreds of men lived and worked at the high Tomboy Mine. Because of the rarified air and strenuous work it is said that these young men's lungs and hearts became the size of watermelons. (Courtesy of Irene R. Visintin and Elvira F. Visintin Wunderlich)

Decorations, bridges, and a doll

Alarge dining room at the Tomboy Mine is festooned for what appears to be a Christmas celebration. Although, the baby doll (center) placed on one of the bridges between the tables suggests that it could have been a setting for a New Year's Eve party instead. (Courtesy of Bill Mahoney)

Up in smoke

Over the years fire torched buildings in almost every mining complex and camp in the San Juans. Here, on July 9, 1922, the Tomboy's main boardinghouse burns while the workers helplessly stare in disbelief. A new smaller structure took its place a few years before the Tomboy shut down. (Photos: Colorado Historical Society, Stephen Hart Library)

CHAPTER THREE: TURBULENCE IN PARADISE (1900s)

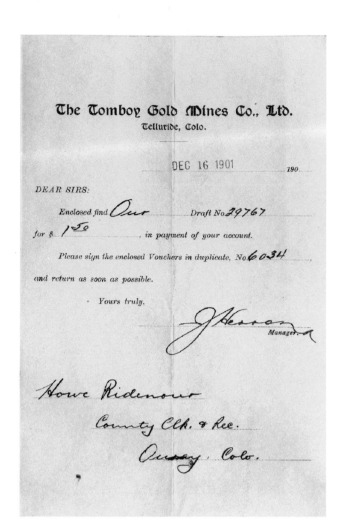

The Tomboy Gold Mines Co., Ltd.
Telluride, Colo.

DEC 16 1901 ___ 190_

DEAR SIRS:

Enclosed find *Our* ___ Draft No. 29767

for $ 1 50 ___ , in payment of your account.

Please sign the enclosed Vouchers in duplicate, No. 6034 ___ ,

and return as soon as possible.

Yours truly,

J Heron
Manager.

Howe Ridenour
County Clk. & Rec.
Ouray, Colo.

Tomboy stationery

The mounds of paperwork necessary to keep the bureaucracy running for a giant mine like the Tomboy generated many white-collar jobs. Integral to the financial success of a mine, experienced mining accountants commanded far better pay than the lowly miners. (Courtesy of P. David Smith)

Billing and shipping clerk

Smartly dressed for his portrait, George A. Nicol worked as a billing and shipping clerk at the Tomboy during the early 1900s. Better a white-collar worker than a miner. Esther Tallman (see page 133) may have seen Nicol during her visit in 1907. (Courtesy of Bill Mahoney)

Tomboy bride

Harriet Fish Backus (above) bequeathed much to Telluride history in her classic work, *Tomboy Bride*. A woman's poignant and insightful account of life at the Tomboy, *Tomboy Bride* (like Lavender's *One Man's West*), is an enjoyable prerequisite to understanding life in turn-of-the-century Telluride and at the high mines. Her words paint a captivating picture of her journey to Telluride, her ascent to the Tomboy, and the excitement and challenge of surviving in a small mining community impossibly situated in the high San Juans. (Telluride Historical Museum)

CHAPTER THREE: TURBULENCE IN PARADISE (1900s)

A Tomboy souvenir

People throughout Colorado dreamed of making the trip to the famous Tomboy Mine. Those lucky enough to fulfill their dream often purchased Tomboy spoons as a memento of their journey. A small mining rail spike and tin cup from the Tomboy also are shown. (Author's photo: Courtesy of Ralph Kemper) (A.E. Buys photos: Author's collection)

CHAPTER THREE: TURBULENCE IN PARADISE (1900s)

12094. LIBERTY BELL MINE, WEST TELLURIDE, COLO.

Liberty Bell gold

Discovered in 1876 at the head of Cornet Creek by an early prospector, W. L. Cornett (the creek clearly being his namesake, minus one "t"), the Liberty Bell remained dormant for almost two decades. After the silver collapse of 1893, however, gold ruled. And gold is what the Liberty had. Two years after the turn of the century, its rock bowels yielded 67,439 tons of gold-bearing ore for an average net profit of one dollar and sixty-two cents a ton. That amounted to $109,251 in tax-free profit.

In this spectacular view the Liberty Bell mining complex clings precariously to the steep slopes far above Telluride. Unfortunately, the Liberty Bell is remembered more for its tragedies than its gold.

Written on the back of the postcard in Swedish is: "Thank you for the card. You cannot believe how slow it has been since you went away. And we did not come to the picnic, but I can go another time." (Postcard: Author's collection)

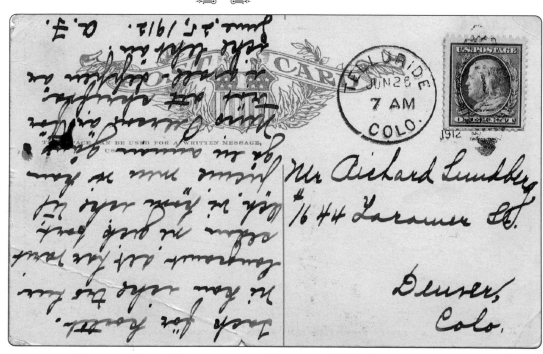

CHAPTER THREE: TURBULENCE IN PARADISE (1900s)

Community room and commissary

Liberty Bell miners probably spent as much leisure time as they could in the confines of the mine's community room and commissary (above). Most of the large and isolated San Juan mines provided recreational and leisure facilities for the miners. Although prostitution was strictly prohibited on mining property, occasionally entrepreneurial ladies erected small houses nearby, no matter how high the elevation. (Telluride Historical Museum)

White death

Given the tragedies that befell it, it is remarkable that the Liberty Bell (its employees are shown below) showed over $100,000 in profits in 1902. On February 28 a massive snowslide came hurtling down Cornet Creek, taking the Liberty Bell's boardinghouse and some bunkhouses. As rescue teams frantically searched for victims, another slide ran, killing two of the rescuers. Then a third slide let go, sweeping more men to their deaths. By the end of the day sixteen men were dead and ten injured. Some of the bodies were not recovered until spring. That summer lightning struck the Liberty Bell's ore-cart rails, electrocuting three workers deep in the mine. (Telluride Historical Museum)

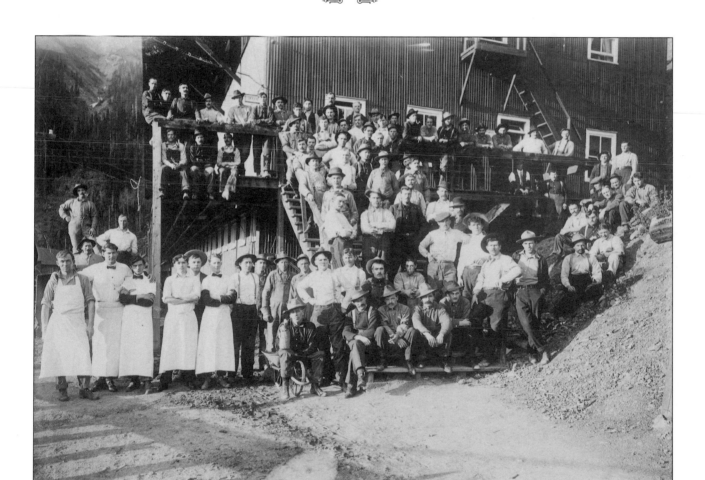

CHAPTER THREE: TURBULENCE IN PARADISE (1900s)

J. D. MILLER, PRESIDENT.
M. D. POTTER, VICE PREST.

JNO. MORTON,
SECRETARY AND GENERAL MANAGER.

J. H. SHOCKLEY, SUPERINTENDENT.
CHAS. CARLTON, AUDITOR.

—THE—

Four Metals Mining Co.

GOLD

SILVER

COPPER

LEAD

GENERAL OFFICES:
17 AND 19 OPERA HOUSE BLOCK, PUEBLO, COLO.
EASTERN OFFICES:
EMPIRE BUILDING, NEW YORK.
FULLERTON BUILDING, ST. LOUIS.
MUTUAL LIFE INS. BUILDING, BOSTON.

OFFICE OF SUPERINTENDENT.

TELLURIDE, COLORADO, 1/26 1901

Other mines and Eastern stock holders

High-profile mines like the Tomboy, Sheridan, Smuggler-Union, and Liberty Bell garner the most attention from historians. Scores of smaller San Juan mines and mining companies, like the Four Metals Mining Company (above), have received scant attention. No matter how large or small the mines, most of their profits ended up in the pockets of Eastern stockholders, always a sore spot with the miners' union. Indeed, few Telluride tears were shed when distant owners lost huge sums of money after backing unproven and undeveloped claims. Note that the Four Metals Mining Co. listed three Eastern offices on its letterhead. (Courtesy of P. David Smith)

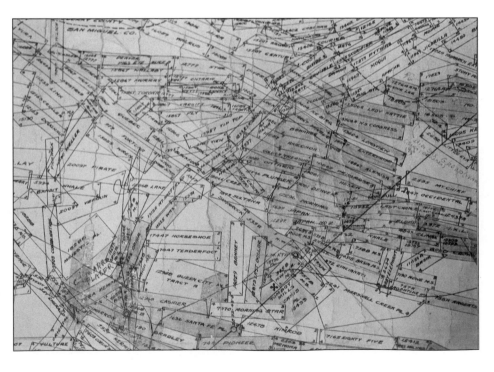

A tangle of claims

Hundreds of overlapping claims created nightmares for claim owners and public record keepers. Many mining lawyers thrived because of legal and technical problems generated by this massive tangle of claims. (Author's photo: Courtesy of Bill Mahoney)

CHAPTER THREE: TURBULENCE IN PARADISE (1900S)

Caring for the sick and injured

Built in 1893 this venerable red sandstone building at the north end of Fir Street served intermittently as a hospital until 1964. Injured miners spent their days convalescing in this homey facility. Those committed with severe "consumption (silicosis)" seldom left alive. The building was commonly known as the Old Miner's Hospital. Mrs. Harriet Fish Backus, author of *Tomboy Bride*, gave birth to the first baby born in the building's confines.

In the early years the most dreaded disease was pneumonia, known as "croupous pneumonia or pneumonitis." Few of the very young or very old survived it. Various strains of Asian flu also proved deadly. During the great influenza epidemic of 1918, long-time resident Alta Cassietto remembers Telluride people "dying like flies." Pneumonia and flu aside, most mining-camp hospitals saw more than their fair share of suffering and death.

Through the years the hospital has closed intermittently. After extensive renovation and preservation work in the mid-1990s, it currently serves as the Telluride Historical Museum. (Telluride Historical Museum)

Miner's Union Hospital

Erected in 1902, as much to spite the mine owners as to care of the sick, the Western Federation of Miners provided the money for this hospital's construction. It only lasted two years, subsequently serving as an American Railway Express Station and, briefly, the local Elks Club. Local legend holds that Robert Livermore, brother-in-law of Bulkeley Wells, once attempted to mail a horse at the express station — and succeeded. This proud three and one-half story brick building with its native stone foundation still stands at the northwest corner of Pine Street and Columbia Avenue. Immediately west (left) of the hospital a two-story residence featured an impressive conical tower. (J. Byers photo: Denver Public Library, Western History Department)

Downtown anchors

For years the plush New Sheridan Hotel and the adjacent two-story Sheridan commercial block on Colorado Avenue anchored downtown Telluride businesses. The New Sheridan's elegant menu offered vichyssoise, fresh strawberries, seafood, possum, pork tenderloin, planked steak, and an excellent variety of California and European wines. Here townspeople line the boardwalk in front of the hotel for a funeral procession. A casket rests in an ornate horse-drawn coach. (Denver Public Library, Western History Department).

Presidential candidates

On July 4, 1903, Presidential candidate William Jennings Bryan repeated his famous "Cross of Gold" speech on a grandstand in front of the New Sheridan Hotel. The eloquent Bryan wanted "free silver." Today the silver vs. gold controversy strikes most people as nothing more than a bit of dull historical fiscal policy. But in turn-of-the-century America it inflamed passions not felt in this country since the Civil War. A year earlier another presidential candidate, Socialist Eugene Debs, pleaded his case in the Sheridan Opera House. (J. Byers and St. Claire photo: Fort Lewis College, Center of Southwest Studies)

CHAPTER THREE: TURBULENCE IN PARADISE (1900s)

Chugging along

During the first decade of the 1900s the Rio Grande Southern chugged along at an even pace. Its main source of revenue, although it never realized substantial profits, continued to be the mining trade. Tourists also rode the little narrow gauge to enjoy the marvelous San Juan scenery, which later became the region's most valuable resource. Many Telluride residents also took weekend excursions to fish at Trout Lake, picnic near Dallas Divide, or view the unique geological formation from which Lizard Head Pass took its name (left). (Courtesy of P. David Smith)

Bucking Snow on the Divide near Telluride, Colo. Lizard Head and Mt. Wilson in distance

Hazards of railroading

Eye-catching scenes like these meant trouble and extra expense for the Rio Grande Southern. Indeed, the more snow, the more financial headaches. And deep snow in the high San Juans is almost a certainty from December through April. Spring brings even more trouble. As the snow melts, meandering creeks become gushing rivers. If the temperatures soar suddenly, as they are prone to do in late spring, the rivers surge violently over their banks with little or no warning. Railroad bridges wash down streams like twisted match sticks. Once rebuilt, the bridges may only last until Fall when they are once again washed out — this time by flash floods caused by enormous cloudbursts (below). (Postcards: Courtesy of Joann and Wes Leech)

175 feet of R. G. Southern Ry. track near Telluride, left 62 feet in the air by a cloud burst

CHAPTER THREE: TURBULENCE IN PARADISE (1900s)

We are having a little cold weather up here now but it is pleasant —

D 4138   Main St. in Winter, looking east, Telluride, Colo.

"We are having a little cold weather up here"

The person who wrote on the postcard (above) did not mind the frigid weather. But winter never did any favors for downtown Telluride. The main street businesses constantly haggled with the city over the best and most efficient method of snow removal. People shoveled the snow into the middle of the wide main street, creating a modern looking two-lane thoroughfare (left). As the snow melted in the spring, Colorado Avenue became a muddy mess. And consider the number of pack animals using Colorado Avenue. Horrid odors and swarms of hungry flies plagued Telluride until early summer when it finally started to dry out. (Postcards: Courtesy of Joann and Wes Leech)

⇥ ⇤

CHAPTER THREE: TURBULENCE IN PARADISE (1900s)

Not high for mountain sheep

By mountain sheep standards this roof was low. It was, however, a good place from which to survey the town of Telluride. Several hundred mountain sheep made their winter homes in San Miguel Park. (Courtesy of Bill Mahoney)

CHAPTER THREE: TURBULENCE IN PARADISE (1900s)

A flood finishes the decade

On September 5, 1909, a powerful cloudburst drenched a precipitous basin above the small settlement of Ames, where years before Lucien Nunn had damned both Hope Lake and Trout Lake to protect his power plant against dry summers. Both dams burst, sending a wall of water and debris rushing down the canyon. Although the torrent of water did not wipe out the power plant, it decimated over a dozen miles of railroad grade along the San Miguel River between Telluride and Placerville.

Without rail service, Telluride once again was forced to rely on pack trains. The first pack train to reach Telluride from Placerville proudly carried a banner broadcasting its precious cargo: Anheuser - Busch beer. It is doubtful that all the townspeople welcomed the now famous beer train, although the patrons of Telluride's thirty-three saloons certainly did. Before the next decade ended, Telluride itself would experience a far more devastating flood. (Courtesy of Walker Collection).

CHAPTER FOUR

FASHIONABLE BALLS, AND FLU (1910S)

Telluride's pristine mountain environment beckoned as much then as now. Riding clubs, picnics in the picturesque mountains, railroad excursions to Trout Lake, and tobboganing in the foothills proved especially popular during the 1910s. In downtown Telluride, Fourth of July parades sporting the talented Silver Cornet Band and shiny horse-drawn fire equipment drew every person in town, or so it seemed, along jam-packed Colorado Avenue. Trains brought in circuses with exotic wonders. Aerialists and acrobats performed daring feats that mesmerized the wide-eyed town folk. And a newfangled four-wheeled riding machine — perceived as utterly hopeless for regularly negotiating the unpredictable mountain roads — created quite a stir when it sputtered onto Colorado Avenue for the first time.

High culture blossomed in this high-altitude mining town as well. The dashing Bulkeley Wells, married to a wealthy British aristocrat and manager of the Smuggler-Union, became "well known for his lavish parties and immaculate dress." The annual Mule Skinners Ball at the Red Men's Hall rated a command performance by the Who's Who of Telluride. In 1914 a new 200-seat opera house was erected next to the Sheridan Hotel. In it, traveling theatre companies and entertainers performed for the rich and famous, and the not so rich and famous. Toward the end of the decade the unbelievable phenomenon of moving pictures flickered before packed houses.

Then came the big flood. Cloudbursts in the high country, especially in late summer, are nothing unusual. Within minutes creeks rise, rivers rush, and dry gulches fill with churning brown water. Yet, one July day in 1914 the cloudbursts seemed to hang on until they became one massive rain storm. Centered high above Cornet Canyon this torrent of water, after swooping up the Liberty Bell Mine waste dump, came crashing down Cornet Creek, smashing the small dam at the foot of the canyon constructed to divert the creek from its natural course. Gaining momentum, this huge volume of brownish-gray sludge with its tumbling trees and boulders surged down Oak Street to Colorado Avenue. Terrified residents barely had time to get out of

THE BIG FLOOD,

the way before this surging mass "filled the lower floors of both the Miner's Union Hospital and the Sheridan Hotel with goo, and left five-foot mats of tangled debris in the central parts of Columbia and Colorado Avenues." Contorted houses littered the hardest hit residential areas. Credit must go to the enterprising and industrious Telluride miners who used powerful fire hoses and a quickly constructed sluice to wash away the deep debris. Astonishingly, only one fatality occurred — a woman was trapped and smothered by mud.

The largest mines in the region continued to show a reasonable profit. In 1915, zinc obtained from the concentrates of the Smuggler-Union brought still more profit, at least to the mine owners. Workers kept improving the roads into the high-country mining basins, better electrified trams shuttled miners and ore alike, and during the winter the Rio Grande Southern plowed through monstrous piles of windblown snow. On Christmas Eve a grand conifer aglow with lights, supplied by power from Lucien Nunn's alternating-current generators, cheered the downtown holiday crowds.

Telluride was not spared the suffering and death of the great influenza epidemic in 1918. It lost about one out of every ten citizens. One eye-witness wrote: "The flu epidemic increased by leaps and bounds and the hospital was full. Additional rooms were opened for hospitalizing the miners who were being brought to Telluride each day. There was a shortage of doctors and nurses and many citizens volunteered to act as nurses for the stricken miners." A second flu epidemic swept the city in 1919.

This decade also saw many of Telluride's young men march off to join the "war to end all wars." Some did not return. Others came back disillusioned. Prior to Armistice Day, November 11, 1918, the citizens of Telluride staged a celebration and "made a dummy of Kaiser Wilhelm and burned it in effigy."

By 1910 the heyday of settlement, expansion, and excitement had passed. Telluride settled comfortably into a small mining town routine. One wonders if the townspeople had any inkling that within two decades most of the mines would be closed and the town largely abandoned.

D 4137 Telluride, Colo., Looking southeast,

Telluride settles in

During this decade Telluride (above) settled comfortably into a small mining town routine. The businesses supplied the mines, the mines supplied the ore, the mills crushed it, and the Rio Grande Southern hauled it. A government publication entitled *All About Colorado (1913)* reported that in 1912 San Miguel County produced $2,400,050 in gold, $717,038 in silver, $339,270 in lead, $251,860 in zinc, and $143,000 in copper.

This same booklet lists Telluride's population as 1,756 and its elevation as 6,744 feet. The 1912 Colorado State Business Directory, however, puts Telluride's population at an even 3,000. A postcard (above) shows Telluride's correct elevation to be considerably higher at 8,756 feet. Whatever the town's population and elevation, almost everyone agreed that it lay in one of the most beautiful valleys in the world. The large building in the foreground (see pages 104 and 105) served as Telluride's grade school and high school. (Postcard: Courtesy of Martin A. Wenger)

A stylish lady

Liveries still constituted a mainstay in the Telluride business community. This stylish lady — shotgun and all — graces a wall advertisement touting the Rogers Brothers' livery, feed and sale stables. One of the brothers also served as mayor. The days that horses and carriages dominated transportation in Telluride, however, were numbered. For it was during this decade when a newfangled four-wheeled riding machine sputtered onto Colorado Avenue, a sure sign of the times to come. (Author's photo: Courtesy of Joann and Wes Leech)

CHAPTER FOUR: FASHIONABLE BALLS, THE BIG FLOOD, AND FLU (1910S)

COMPLIMENTS OF
BELMONT BAR
JOHNSON & JOHNSON
Phone, Black 685
TELLURIDE, COLO.

Tobogganing in Telluride

The Belmont Bar featured tobogganing, a popular Telluride pastime, on its 1911 calendar. Decades later, an unusual fate awaited the bar. "Next to the jail [South Spruce Street] and back a bit is the old Belmont [Hotel and Bar]. The Belmont used to be at the edge of the street, but the property belonged to the Masonic Temple, and the lodge wanted the building torn down. George Kovich, the owner who was then 70, sawed the building in half and moved the structure back onto his own land . . . " (Fetter and Fetter, 1979). Unfortunately, neither half remains. (Author's photo: Courtesy of Joann and Wes Leech)

Mule Skinners Ball Committee

On March 10, 1911, the Mule Skinners Ball Committee gathered in the Improved Order of Red Men's Hall on South Fir Street. A painted Venetian scene adorns the curtain. Champagne and wine bottles nearly outnumber the committee, while a dog rests on the lap of a man seated on stage. The overall appearance and demeanor of this group suggests that it may have been a rung or two beneath the social creme de la creme of Telluride. (J. Byers photo: Denver Public Library, Western History Department)

CHAPTER FOUR: FASHIONABLE BALLS, THE BIG FLOOD, AND FLU (1910s)

Uptown establishment

Located on Colorado Avenue between the Telluride Bank and Roma Cafe, the Telluride Beer Hall catered to a "good brand of customer." Schlitz and Coors beer signs frame the entrance. Seldom seen in drinking establishments, several potted plants flourish behind the left window. (Courtesy of Irene R. Visintin and Elvira F. Visintin Wunderlich)

Caesar

This rare view of the interior of the Telluride Beer Hall spotlights a classic upright gaming piece: a Mills Owl Floor Machine manufactured between 1897 and 1918. Resting next to the upright slot machine is Caesar. According to sisters Irene Visintin and Elvira Visintin Wunderlich (the owner's daughter-in-law), when Caesar sensed that a fight was brewing between

customers, he would bark fiercely, preventing most fisticuffs. A careless neighbor accidently poisoned Caesar. (Courtesy of Irene R. Visintin and Elvira F. Visintin Wunderlich)

Another high class establishment

Rows of cylinder whiskey bottles line several high shelves behind the bar. This saloon is also believed to be the Telluride Beer Hall. Heads of two mountain sheep hang on either side of a mule deer head. On the floor to the left is a miner's tin lunch bucket. Three spittoons sit between the bar and the foot railing. Small wonder few women frequented this bar. Prohibition would soon force all drinking establishments in Telluride to close, although that is not to say that whiskey became impossible to obtain. (Telluride Historical Museum)

Section hands

In this tattered photograph ten section hands take a break from their work. The young man on the left holds a spike puller. Freshly turned gravel in the foreground indicates they may have been either leveling or aligning track. The old storage tank's unique support configuration, visible behind the man holding the spike puller, identifies this scene as the Rio Grande Southern yard in Telluride. (Courtesy of Ralph Kemper)

Rio Grande Southern money

Perhaps this check dated July 10, 1914, bought some of the equipment for the section hands shown on this page. The Rio Grande Southern's stylish vignette in the upper left hand corner adorned much of the railroad's paperwork. A few weeks after this check was issued, a catastrophic flood forced section hands to labor even harder and longer hours to clear mounds of mud from the tracks near downtown Telluride. (Author's photo: Courtesy of Scott Strain)

"At certain seasons the falls impress you"

"While Bridal Veil Falls is the acme of scenic beauty, we have many others of nature's glorious water falls of minor importance, yet very interesting withal. The next in interest, perhaps, is Cornet Falls [above], which dashes its waters almost within the corporate limits of the Town of Telluride. The waters of Cornet Creek at this point are thrown over a perpendicular precipice of red sandstone rock nearly 200 feet in height. The creek and falls are buried deep in a narrow canon and, therefore, do not attract wide attention, although, at certain seasons the falls impress you as worthy of high place or rank among the scenic wonders of the world" (*Telluride and San Miguel County,* 1894). (J. Byers photo: Courtesy of Martin A. Wenger)

CHAPTER FOUR: FASHIONABLE BALLS, THE BIG FLOOD, AND FLU (1910S)

A massive cloudburst

Cloudbursts in San Juan country, especially in late summer, are nothing unusual. Within minutes creeks rise, rivers rush, bone-dry gulches fill with churning water. Yet on the 27th day of July, 1914, a continuous cloudburst spawned torrential rain. Centered high above Cornet Canyon this torrent of water, after swooping up the Liberty Bell Mine waste dump, came crashing down Cornet Creek. It smashed the small dam at the foot of the canyon constructed to divert the creek from its natural course. Gaining momentum, the immense cascade of brownish-gray sludge filled with tumbling trees and boulders tore down Oak Street to Colorado Avenue (above). (Courtesy of Joann and Wes Leech)

Terrified residents

Terrified residents barely had time to get out of the way. Miraculously, only one fatality occurred. Vera Blakeley dashed back into her home to retrieve her dog, only to be trapped and smothered by debris. In this scene shocked residents begin to search through the deep, gummy mud for personal belongings. (Courtesy of P. David Smith)

Contorted houses

Contorted houses littered the hardest hit residential areas. The force of the surging mass of debris and mud knocked homes off their foundations, twisting and turning them like doll houses. People must have watched in horror as this beautiful home on North Oak Street spun off its foundation and nearly fell apart. (Courtesy of P. David Smith)

"This is all mud and rocks that came thro the market"

Martin G. Wenger scribbled a telling description on one of the photographs taken immediately after the flood. (Courtesy of Martin A. Wenger)

Cleaning up

Industrious and efficient Telluride miners used powerful fire hoses (right) and a hastily constructed sluice (below right) to wash away the deep debris. Few other towns in Colorado could have so quickly garnered the resources and expertise necessary to handle the terrible aftermath of the flood. According to Irene Visintin and Elvira Visintin Wunderlich, a "Flood Relief Committee" was formed to accept donations from Telluride and the surrounding towns. Donations poured in. "The Wunderlich's received $250 and Visintin's $100."

The owners of the Phoenix Market (above) quickly hung a new sign, signalling that they were back in business. The Smuggler-Union employment office can be seen to the left of the market. To the right of the market curious women and children watch

the cleanup from the boardwalk. Two signs, "Transient Rooms" and "Smith's Rooming House," hang above their heads. A couple of well-dressed men watch the clean-up proceedings. (J. Byers photos: Fort Lewis College, Center of Southwest Studies)

CHAPTER FOUR: FASHIONABLE BALLS, THE BIG FLOOD, AND FLU (1910s)

"The most brilliantly lighted town, perhaps, in the world"

By 1919, when some Eastern cities still considered street lights a novelty, Telluride had sported well-lit streets for nearly three decades. As early as 1894 a Telluride Board of Trade pamphlet boasted: "Telluride is the most brilliantly lighted town, perhaps, in the world. Under a recent agreement with the town board, five arc lights of 1,500 candle power each, are to be immediately erected on Colorado Avenue, the main business street of the town. This will give the town an aggregate of nearly 9,000 candle power consumed on the streets alone."

As shown by this image, Telluride's tradition of electrical pioneering continued into the 1910s. "Irrigate by Electricity and Save Money" exhorts the sign on the power company's impressive model. Motors and pumps powered by electricity forced the water to the top of the display, then sent it cascading down a series of sluice-like steps. What better demonstration of the potency of electricity for mine owners and farmers alike? And what more unlikely place for the age of electricity to arrive? (Fort Lewis College, Center of Southwest Studies)

A Telluride tradition

In 1916, at the corner of Fir Street and Colorado Avenue, townspeople gathered around a lighted Christmas tree to celebrate Christmas and "distribute community presents." A piano placed by the tree indicates that community carolling constituted part of the festive activities.

In the lower left of the photograph men in a horse-drawn sleigh full of wooden barrels and boxes observe the proceedings. Baisch Drugstore and Jewelry Company must have enjoyed added business during these special holiday gatherings. (Fort Lewis College, Center of Southwest Studies)

Aglow in the night

Telluride's grand conifer aglow with radiant lights maintains its holiday vigil on deserted Colorado Avenue. (Fort Lewis College, Center of Southwest Studies)

CHAPTER FOUR: FASHIONABLE BALLS, THE BIG FLOOD, AND FLU (1910S)

An electric range parade

How appropriate that the "electrical capitol of the world" would stage a parade featuring the new cooking rage — electric ranges. According to the caption written on this 1917 photograph, these two wagons with ranges (some in crates, others displayed) are part of an electric range parade making its way toward Colorado Avenue. What incredible inventions had Lucien Nunn's alternating current wrought? (Fort Lewis College, Center of Southwest Studies)

Tower of power

Mounted atop 13,114-foot Imogene Pass, a tower of power helped carry Lucien Nunn's alternating current to the Camp Bird Mine. "Management of the mine at Camp Bird found that it was cheaper to build power lines to connect with L. L. Nunn's alternating-current network than it was to operate their own direct-current plant" (Collman, McCoy, and Graves, 1994).

Engineers designed unique crossarms to hold the insulators. "This arrangement of insulators allowed each to withstand its share of the strain caused by high winds, and the hinge arrangement of the crossarm provided for swaying during wind storms" (McDougald, 1997). Viewed from a distance these crossarms do not strike one as substantial. Up close they are more impressive. The crossarm shown here, retrieved from Imogene Pass decades ago, measures close to eight feet and weighs more than fifty pounds. (Fort Lewis College, Center of Southwest Studies) (Author's photo: Author's collection)

Noisy and impractical

Besides attracting a large and curious crowd, the first motorized vehicle to sputter down Colorado Avenue spooked several horses. The noisy contraption was judged as too fragile for rugged mountain roads. Few townspeople expected to see another. According to the caption written on this old photograph, Charles F. Loebnitz of Telluride sits at the helm of an early Oldsmobile (1904-1906) curved-dash runabout with wood spokes, solid rubber tires, and steering handle. (Telluride Historical Museum)

Crossarms and insulators

"**J**uly, 1915, chained up [and] collecting wood," reads the description on the back of this photograph. Chained up, yes. Collecting wood, no. This man surely worked for the Telluride Power Company. Carefully aligned power-pole crossarms lay across lengthy poles on either side of the bed of this vehicle (possibly a Dodge Brothers) with an atypically long hood. Large ceramic insulators — also indicating a power line — rest helter skelter on the crossarms. The poles are most likely tools for propping up poles or manipulating "hot" wire during insulator removal. With the long poles blocking both doors, it appears this man had to exit his canvas-topped vehicle by crawling out one of the windows. (Fort Lewis College, Center of Southwest Studies)

Phone business

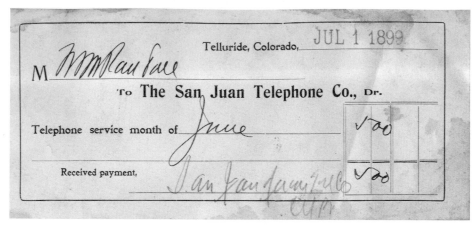

Phone business fast became big business in Telluride. This early receipt shows that it cost customers five dollars a month (or sixty dollars a year) for local phone service in the remote mining camp. All the large mines immediately had phone wires strung to their headquarters high in the mountains. Below timber line, trees often served as poles. Even today it is not unusual to find a side pin for a small glass telephone insulator still nailed to a long-fallen tree. (Courtesy of P. David Smith)

A visual icon of early 20th century America

Female phone operators wired to their switchboards by headsets is one of the more familiar visual icons of the early 20th century. Here young Telluride women, their voices more familiar than their faces, handle local and long-distant phone calls. It was one of the few respectable jobs for women in Telluride. During late winter and early spring avalanches often wiped out telephone poles and line, interrupting service for days. (Telluride Historical Museum)

"Easter egg distribution"

Decked out in their Easter bonnets and holiday apparel, a large gathering of Telluride children assembled for a photograph on Colorado Avenue. Formal "Easter egg distributions" exemplified Telluride's sense of community during the 1910s. For years Telluride's social and cultural leaders encouraged and oversaw community events like these. Though only a block away, young and old East Pacific Avenue denizens, especially those of the infamous "Popcorn Alley," seldom participated in Telluride's "legitimate" social events. The Byers Photographic Studio and the Sheridan Annex can be seen in the left background. (Telluride Historical Museum)

CHAPTER FOUR: FASHIONABLE BALLS, THE BIG FLOOD, AND FLU (1910s)

Knights in uniform

A plethora of secret and benevolent societies existed in most mining towns. Telluride was no exception, with over a dozen societies listed in the 1915 Colorado State Business Directory. Here members of the Knights Templar are dressed in their prized regalia for Easter, 1910. (Telluride Historical Museum)

Elks Club Christmas

This 1910 photograph shows the festive Elks Club Christmas decorations in their early headquarters (later they occupied the First National Bank building) above the H. C. Baisch Drugstore. One member of the club has donned a complete Santa Claus outfit. Most likely the piles of oranges and presents were made ready for the children. An ornate coal-burning heater (right foreground) kept the room warm. (Telluride Historical Museum)

Snowbound in Ophir

Keeping the tracks open for the Rio Grande Southern also demanded extraordinary vigilance and effort. A postcard from Ames bearing the initials "M. M." describes a giant winter storm during February of 1910. Based on the number of smoke columns, the photograph on the postcard captures a rotary plow — with three locomotives supplying additional power — cleaning deep snow off the tracks "a little above the [Ophir] Loop." (Courtesy of Jerry O'Rourke)

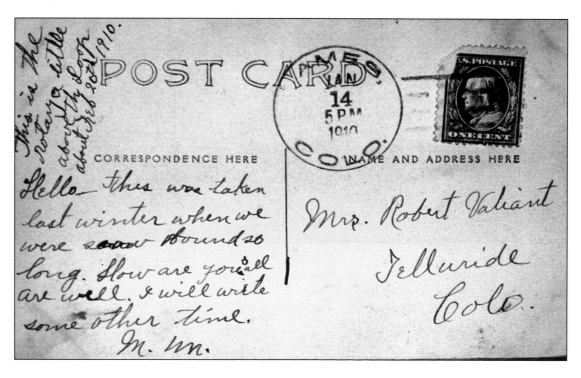

Damaging snowstorms

On January 31, 1914, "one of the most destructive snowstorms which has visited this section of the country in the past 12 years started-in last week, stopping passenger traffic on the Rio Grande Southern Railroad from the south (between here [Telluride] and Durango) for several days. . . . The weather, for a couple of days, reminded one of the big snowstorm 12 years ago — February 28, 1902 — the time of the destructive and death-dealing storm, when the Liberty Bell snowslides ran and caused a loss of life and temporary damage to the mining interests. . . . Then, 19 years ago, there was a similar storm . . . " (quoted from *The Examiner* in Collman, McCoy, and Graves, 1993).

Here a Rio Grande Southern rotary snowplow creates a moving white arc on May 2, 1919, near Vance Junction, southeast of Telluride. Telluride and the mining industry relied heavily on the services, however irregular, of the Rio Grande Southern. While most winter storms could, in time, be dealt with, there was nothing Telluride nor the Rio Grande Southern could do to clear the economic storm clouds gathering on the horizon. (M. Toinolli photo: Fort Lewis College, Center of Southwest Study)

Deadly revival attempt

In 1925, a small group of Scandinavian colleagues took a "cleanup lease" on the Black Bear Mine far above Telluride in Imogene Basin (one basin south of Savage Basin). Years earlier Joseph Byers photographed the Black Bear stamp mill and boardinghouse with Ajax Peak in the background (above). The revival attempt ended abruptly in 1926 when two of the Scandinavians (Ed and Marie Rajala) perished in an avalanche. (J. Byers photo: Courtesy of the Ouray County Museum)

WAGES PAID JANUARY 1923. at THE SMUGGLER & UNION MINE, SMUGGLER, COLORADO.			
Stoping Machine Men	4.50	Shaft Men	5.50
Leyner Machine Men	4.75	Track Men	4.50
Timbermen	4.50	Pump Men	4.25
Timbermen Helpers	4.00	Pipe Men	4.25
Chute Blasters	4.50	Hoist Men	4.75
Nippers	4.50	Compressor Men	4.50
Muckers & Trammers	4.00	Samplers	4.50
Cagers	5.00	Crusher Men	4.00
Ore Sorters	4.00	Dumpers	4.00
Old Stope Miners	5.00	Yard Men	3.50
Stope Cleaners	5.10	Laborers	3.50
Motormen	4.30	Watchmen	4.00
Loaders	4.00	Shift Bosses	6.25 & Bonus
Powder Monkeys	4.25		

High country wages

This original 1923 Smuggler-Union Mine wage scale from Smuggler, Colorado, lists miners' daily wages. The names of the jobs themselves — including "Powder Monkeys," "Nippers," and "Old Stope Miners" — also tell about the elaborate division of labor down in the mines. Above ground, men like these (below), who probably worked as cooks, butchers, waiters, and dishwashers, earned even less.

In Telluride wages varied widely. For example, in 1927 a young Alta Cassietto started work as a reporter for *The Journal* for $10 a week. Years later when she became manager her pay increased to $125 a month. (Courtesy of Bill Ellicott) (Courtesy of Walker Collection)

CHAPTER FIVE: HARD TIMES, BUT GOOD TIMES (1920s-1940s)

Robin Hood or Scoundrel?

Telluride struggled to survive after the closure of the Tomboy, Smuggler, and scores of other mines. When the stock market collapsed in 1929, it was too much for the small mining town. Telluride's population quickly plummeted to less than 600. To prevent a rush of creditors, the Bank of Telluride temporarily closed it doors in September 1929. Hardworking Telluride citizens — like people throughout America — lost their life savings overnight.

Before the Bank of Telluride closed, its colorful and high-profile president, Charles (Buck) Waggoner (on the left in center photograph) arranged a visual demonstration of his bank's assets and used stylish models in his ads (right). The hand guns laying on the table were as much for show as security. When it became clear to Waggoner that he could not keep his bank afloat, he concocted a complicated financial scheme that involved defrauding some large New York financial institutions. Some historians claim that Waggoner's financial conspiracy was an effort to repay his friends in town, others says he did it for himself. Two things are certain, Waggoner ended up in jail and the Bank of Telluride folded in 1929. Three decades would pass before it opened again. (Courtesy of Joann and Wes Leech) (Courtesy of Walker Collection) (Telluride Historical Museum)

SECTION ONE   THE DENVER POST—FIRST IN EVERYTHING—   3

TELLURIDE ALL AGOG OVER GOLD HIGHGRADING CASE

THEY'RE TALKING ABOUT CHARGES WHEREVER PEOPLE CONGREGATE

Arrests and Allegations Provide Town in Fabulously Rich San Juan Area Most Excitement Since Waggoner Bank Incident of 1929.

SCENES AND PRINCIPALS IN HIGHGRADING CASE

Twelve men were under charges Saturday in connection with what Telluride authorities say is the biggest highgrading case in the state's history—the theft of between $50,000 and $100,000 worth of gold from the Smuggler-Union and Tomboy mines. Telluride officials say those under arrest were involved in the buying or marketing of gold obtained from miners employed at the mines. Sev-

eral of the principals in the case are shown here. Sheriff Guy Warrick of San Miguel county says the "highgraded" ore was "concentrated" and prepared for sale on the market—to smelters, dental supply houses, jewelry shops and other buyers of new and old gold. The accused men will be arraigned at Telluride Friday and hearings will probably be held in April.

"Largest highgrading case in the state's history"

Barely ten years after the Waggoner scandal, another scandal erupted. Sheriff Lawrence E. Warrick arrested a ring of Telluride highgraders — miners who smuggled rich pieces of ore out of the mines. The *Denver Post* reported that the theft of "$50,000 to $100,000 worth of gold" from the Smuggler-Union and the Tomboy made it the "largest highgrading case in the state's history." (Courtesy of Eileen Brown)

Sheriff Guy Warrick of Telluride is shown at his desk. Beside him stands Joe Clementi of Ophir, one of the twelve defendants in the highgrading case.

CHAPTER FIVE: HARD TIMES, BUT GOOD TIMES (1920s-1940s)

Even the priest left town

By the mid 1930s Telluride's population dropped below 500. Even the priest left town and Telluride "again became a mission of Montrose sixty-five miles away. There were no paved roads, and no regular mass was held. The solitude of the 1880s fell upon the town . . . The Pick & Gad, Idle House, Big Swede, and the cribs were still open, but the main street was a far cry from the exuberant days of the bullwackers, mule trains, and celebrating miners on a binge" (Fetter and Fetter, 1979).

Built in 1896, St. Patrick's Catholic Church stands vacant at the corner of Galena Avenue and North Spruce Street. Years earlier, long curls prevailed (below) in the "First Communion Class — 1913." This section of town became known as "Catholic Hill" because of the large number of Catholic Italians and Austrians who lived there. Refurbished and once again beckoning the faithful, St. Patrick's still stands on its original location on Catholic Hill. (Denver Public Library, Western History Department) (Courtesy of Bill Ellicott)

First Communion Class — 1913

CHAPTER FIVE: HARD TIMES, BUT GOOD TIMES (1920s-1940s)

School transportation

By the late 1920s school buses began service for children from Pandora (above). This "motorized coach with back and front doors" transported them to school in Telluride. Chester Lee drove Telluride's first motorized school bus. (Telluride Historical Museum)

Champions of the hard courts

The caption scribbled on the back of this photograph reads: "1935, Telluride High School Basketball Team." W. L. Nardin served as coach. But notice the "T.F.D." on the players' shirts. Could this be the Telluride Fire Department's team instead? If so, why are they holding a trophy basketball with the high school's monogram? (H. Reid photo: Courtesy of Arlene Reid)

1. Marie Michel, 2 Ida Lepin, 3 Flossie Crandall, 4 Susan Mathews 5. ...
6 Irene Hendrickson, 7 Nellie O'Kelly
coach Ferris   Dons Toddy

Girls played too

The members of Telluride High School's girls basketball team aligned themselves according to height for this photograph. Their modest uniforms were in keeping with the Victorian social climate of the times, but they must have encumbered athletic movements on the court. One wonders why the coach had the Teddy Bear, probably the team's mascot, in chains. (Telluride Historical Museum)

Changing steel

In the 1930s Fourth of July still meant spirited parades and contests in Telluride, no matter how depleted the population or depressed the economy. "Double-jacking" drilling contests proved especially popular. Here, one man (Jack Figler) wields the eight-pound sledge while another holds the steel drill. "Changing steel" involved pitching a dull drill — notice the drill flying through the air — and quickly replacing it with a smaller, sharper drill without missing a stroke. (Courtesy of Jerry O'Rourke)

Mining the dumps

During the 1930s and 1940s independent mining contractors arranged to rework old mill tailings. Shown here is a contractor's "slusher bucket" scooping up discarded ore from the old Tomboy dump. Money could still be made by trucking ore down to the huge "Red Mill" in Pandora, where refined ore-processing techniques yielded valuable base metals and gold. Here a small shed harbors, and partially hides, an unlikely power supply for the slusher bucket: a late 1920s Model A Ford truck. Its four-speed transmission probably fit its winching duties well. (Courtesy of Jerry O'Rourke)

CHAPTER FIVE: HARD TIMES, BUT GOOD TIMES (1920s-1940s)

Reworking the cone dump

A tunnel into the Cimarron Mine's loose, cone-shaped tailings pile required extensive cribbing. It also created a lunar looking landscape. One of the workers parked his 1941 Ford pickup truck near the bore. Reworking old tailings piles yielded enough precious minerals to keep several small, independent contractors in business. (Courtesy of Jerry O'Rourke)

Portable air compressors and mucking machines

Independent mining contractors also took out leases to work the larger mines, like the Pennsylvania Mine shown here. Attached to the rear of a Jeffrey mining locomotive is a portable air compressor and receiving tank (above). It provided compressed air for operating the drill on the "mucking machine" (below). One miner (barely visible to the right) stands on a small foothold on the side of the mucking machine. From there he operated the drill with two handles — one moving it forward, the other back. Once the cart on the mucking machine was full, it tipped backwards, dumping the ore onto the tunnel floor or into a waiting ore cart.

Of this work Lavender (1943) wrote: "A good machineman can drill about fifteen holes five feet deep, or a total of seventy-five feet, in a shift. This doesn't give him much time for admiring the scenery. He stops only to change dull steel for sharp or adjust his machine. Jets of air and water forced through the hollow steel clean out the cuttings and reduce the deadly rock dust which shreds your lungs, producing silicosis, the grim reaper of the mines." (Photos courtesy of Jerry O'Rourke)

CHAPTER FIVE: HARD TIMES, BUT GOOD TIMES (1920s-1940s)

Gyro crusher and ore carts

Next the ore would be dumped into a shaft leading to a gyro crusher (above). Once the crusher did its work, the ore slid down into another set of mining carts (below) that transported the valuable cargo to trucks. The trucks hauled the ore to the mills below.

Larger pieces of ore frequently got "hung up" in the ore shoot above the gyro crusher. To free the jam miners used long iron prods and shovels to get the ore moving again. The miner driving the trolley engine in the bottom photograph should have been wearing a hard hat. (Photos courtesy of Jerry O'Rourke)

CHAPTER FIVE: HARD TIMES, BUT GOOD TIMES (1920s-1940s)

Hauling less ore past larger toxic tailings ponds

With Bridal Veil Falls in the background, a Rio Grande Southern train with a Denver and Rio Grande engine chugs out of Pandora toward Telluride. Ore shipments decreased substantially during the 1930s and 1940s. The ore shipped from the great Red Mill in Pandora usually ended up at large smelters in Durango.

Like giant paramecia, toxic tailings ponds from the Pandora mills stretched west toward Telluride. Cyanide, mercury, and other toxic substances permeated these ponds, percolating into the soil and water beneath them. Today this series of poisonous ponds has been reclaimed, meaning the toxic material has been "cleansed." The remains of the pond sites are now covered with grass. And trout once again thrive in the San Miguel River below. (O. D. Perry photo: Denver Public Library, Western History Department) (H. Reid photo: Courtesy of Jerry O'Rourke)

CHAPTER FIVE: HARD TIMES, BUT GOOD TIMES (1920s-1940s)

Downtown Telluride hangs on

Bootlegging helped Telluride survive during the Great Depression. Tons of sugar was shipped in, legal or not. Despite all the laws and ordinances forbidding the "production or sale" of hard liquor, it flowed freely in several back rooms. Most of the townspeople simply looked the other way. They knew Telluride needed bootleg liquor to survive. "Prohibition was stupid anyway," one liberal old-timer rationalized. (Courtesy of Walker Collection)

Allen's dental office

The draconian dental equipment in Dr. Charles Allen's downtown office suggests the treatment might have been worse than the ache. Not so, testified one long-time Telluride resident: "Dr. Allen fixed up many a sore tooth real good, including mine." A pair of tanned coyote hides adorn the couch. (Telluride Historical Museum)

Telluride's only doctor

To the relief of the townspeople, Dr. Joe Parker (above) arrived in Telluride in 1932. He served as the only medical doctor in the economically depressed Telluride region until 1947. By all accounts Joe Parker, who obtained his medical degree from the University of Colorado in 1931, was a fine human, physician, and community leader.

Stories still circulate about many of the challenges he faced. For example, Fetter and Fetter (1979) wrote: "The hospital used a form of anesthesia known as the 'drip-mask' method, which used ether dripped onto a piece of folded gauze held over the patient's nose. It was safer than chloroform but not without risk, especially when the power failed. The danger of explosion was too great to use a kerosene lamp, so Dr. Parker rapidly became skilled at performing surgery, delivering babies, and setting fractures in the dark." (Courtesy of Dr. James Parker)

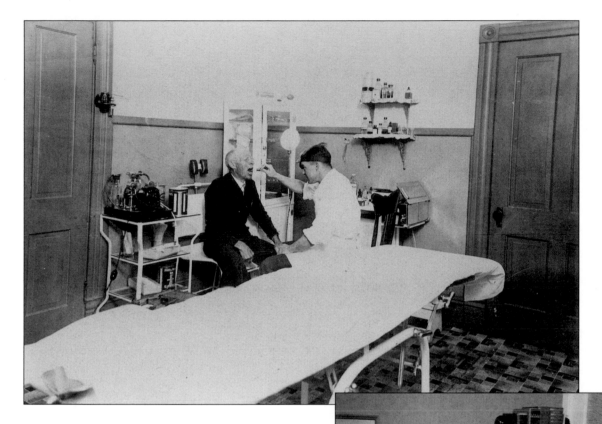

Still in the family

During the early years a room in the Parker home on Colorado Avenue served as his office (above). Here he uses a tongue depressor to examine Dan Hanlon's throat. Not everyone could afford to pay cash for his services. "One man paid an $85 bill with rabbits — valued at three for a $1" (Wright, 1974). The small table to the left of the patient and the upright medicine chest in the corner are now in his son's (Dr. James Parker) examination office in Grand Junction, Colorado (right).

As for the local hospital: "Nothing in the hospital met the standards of the Colorado Health Department. The state's inspector, a Mrs. East, regularly threatened to close the place and Dr. Parker agreed each time it would be a good idea. The hospital consistently operated at a deficit, averaging about $1,000 monthly" (Wright, 1974). (Courtesy of Dr. James Parker) (Author's photo: Courtesy of Dr. James Parker)

A crib for the doctor

Some of the mines reopened in the late 1930s. The Argentine Mine in Rico hired Dr. Joe Parker for $400 a month to make a weekly trip to Rico. Each Thursday afternoon he would tend to the medical needs of the mine's two hundred employees and their families. Later the Argentine Mine reimbursed Dr. Parker based on a capitation method. For example, each miner would have $1 a month deducted from his salary to pay the doctor's salary. If there were 150 miners employed, the doctor would receive $150. But, the doctor had to pay for all medical supplies. So some months, when few miners needed medicines and supplies, Dr. Parker earned money. Other months, when several miners needed medicines and supplies, Dr. Parker lost money. His son points out that this was probably one of the first, and still controversial, medical capitation plans in the United States.

As a gesture of appreciation for all Dr. Parker had done for them, some of the miners in Telluride winched a vacant crib onto a flatbed truck and hauled it up to Trout Lake, located about half way between Telluride and Rico. This provided Dr. Parker with a place to rest during the trip, or to wait out bad weather. He also liked to fish. Today it still serves as the Parker family's vacation home. Pictured above are Dr. Joe Parker, and his son, Tim, leaning against their 1949 Mercury in front of their cabin at Trout Lake. "'I worked like crazy,' Dr. Parker remembers, 'We [his wife was a nurse] only expected to stay two or three years, but it took 15 years to get enough money to leave'" (Wright, 1974). (Courtesy of Dr. James Parker)

Trouble below

Dr. Joe Parker (left), who also served as Telluride's coroner (not to mention a stint as mayor, president of the local school board, City Health Officer, County Coroner, deputy sheriff, and volunteer fireman), and Don McNaughton, a mine inspector, stand at the Butterfly #3 Mine south of Telluride. According to Dr. Parker's son, the presence of his father and the mine inspector together meant that a miner probably died in an accident below. "Most accidents occurred on the night shift. The miners didn't sleep as soundly during the daytime, and they'd become fatigued from prolonged sleeplessness" (Wright, 1974). (Courtesy of Dr. James Parker and Bill Mahoney)

Telluride languishes

During the 1930s and 1940s Telluride languished. Its population threatened to drop below 400, yet it had a comforting small-town rhythm. During the summer a few tourists, railroad buffs, and amateur historians visited the remote mining camp. A mine or two might open, some independent contractor might hit a rich pocket or two, and some bad whiskey might send a few imbibers to the hospital. As witnessed by the image above, during winter the town went into a deep freeze. Few tourists came.

Occasionally indoor bazaars and dinners were held in the high school and the courthouse. Mining activity, even though underground, seemed to subside as well.

An electric sign advertising one of the local movie theatres hangs above Harry Miller's barber pole on Colorado Avenue. Visible over the snow banks are the distinctive and familiar towers of the Elks Club (formerly First National Bank) and the San Miguel County Courthouse. (Courtesy of Ogda Matson Walter and Roger Polley)

Dressed to cut

Harry Miller, one of the local barbers, always wore a suit and tie to work. To shave customers he used a straight-edged razor like this one, etched with the name "Telluride."

During Telluride's economically depressed times, one amateur historian described the town as: " . . . a good-sized place, and, although some of its buildings are empty and certain blocks toward the edge of the city look dilapidated, the heart of the town is full of stores, and the streets close to the main thoroughfare are full of homes surrounded by gardens and shaded by trees" (Wolle, 1949). (Author's photo: Courtesy of Dan MacKendrick)

High fashion

Local women model fashionable apparel at the grand opening of Viola's Dress Shop in downtown Telluride. Wearing a flower corsage, Viola Warrick (far right) oversees the festive occasion. (Courtesy of Eileen Brown)

CHAPTER FIVE: HARD TIMES, BUT GOOD TIMES (1920s-1940s)

A modest beginning

In the 1930s some locals paid five dollars to join a local ski club. They strapped on their long wooden skis, grabbed onto a short rope tow on the snowy slope (bottom image dates to the early 1960s) of Grizzly Gulch near downtown, and skied back down the hill. In 1938 Jack Mahoney (left) flies through the air with almost the greatest of ease. His brother Bill Mahoney, a member of the Colorado Ski Hall of Fame, oversaw the development of Joe Zoline's now famous Telluride ski area. Bill "Senior" Mahoney has astutely gathered and preserved numerous old photographs of historic Telluride. (Photos courtesy of Bill Mahoney)

Zulu Run

In the late 1930s former Telluride resident Martin G. Wenger learned that his young brother, Herbert, was a "bit down and out." So Martin invited him to work his unpatented Zulu claim during the summer. (The name "Zulu" came to Martin many years earlier while reading a book about Africa.) While attending college Martin's son, Martin Jr., spent his summer breaks helping his uncle work the mine. They lived in a tiny one-room cabin (above) from May through September for several summers.

The mine was located high above Telluride and the only persons they saw were "United States Geological Survey employees and a power line walker." Once a month "they would hike to town and rent a horse to haul up supplies." They obtained water by melting portions of a big snow drift. Now, every winter thousands of people ski down "Zulu Queen," where the Wenger cabin once stood. (Courtesy of Martin A. Wenger)

Skiing near Dallas Divide

A caravan of skiers' cars (below) line the road near the summit of Dallas Divide. Dr. Joe Parker's car, parked in the foreground, displays the "50 50" on his license plate. The first "50" indicates that San Miguel County ranked 50th in population (out of 52 counties) in Colorado. Dr. Parker added the second "50" claiming, tongue in cheek, that patients who came to him had a "50 — 50" chance.

In the top image, another Telluride ski-pioneer, Bruce Palmer, clears a barbwire fence on Dallas Divide. (Photos courtesy of Dr. James Parker)

A horse-drawn sleigh

Some Parker family members and friends ready themselves for a sleigh ride through the streets of Telluride on Christmas day in the mid-1940s. (Courtesy of Dr. James Parker)

Western Colo. Power Co's. Relief Station

Horizontal snow

"Snow hardly ever seemed to come out of the sky, just came howlin' straight across. Couldn't see a thing. Cold too, terrible cold." Words of Ogda Walter describing her winter years as a young girl at the 12,000 feet Tomboy Mine. Imagine, then, being stationed at the Western Colorado Power Company's station on top of 13,100 foot Imogene Pass. (Fort Lewis College, Center of Southwest Studies)

Avalanches

Avalanches continually plagued the mines, power companies, and railroads. Costly, and sometimes deadly, avalanches never seemed to give fair warning. Besides the fatal slides at the Liberty Bell in 1902 and the Black Bear in 1926, the Ajax slide in 1928 claimed two more lives, one of them a woman. In this scene a group of curious locals inspect the aftermath of an avalanche that buried the Rio Grande Southern tracks near Ophir. (Telluride Historical Museum)

Anatomy of a snowslide

The crest of snow (upper right) where the slide broke loose is about fifteen feet high. A Western Power Company employee cautiously inspects a downed power line. Potential for slides increases when deep snow accumulates over a layer of frozen snow. When the snow on top becomes heavy enough, it literally slides off the frozen layer beneath it.

As these massive chunks of snow start charging down the mountain, they reach velocities that exceed 200 miles per hour. Smashed trees, boulders, hunks of buildings become part of the hurtling, deadly mass. Little remains standing in their wake. (Fort Lewis College, Center of Southwest Studies)

CHAPTER FIVE: HARD TIMES, BUT GOOD TIMES (1920s-1940s)

Imagine the shock

Imagine the shock one spring day in the early 1970s when Bill and Steve Wenger returned to their sturdy cabin above Alta Lakes. Only the foundation remained. Where was the rest of the cabin? Smashed to pieces and scattered down the slope by a powerful snowslide. Now consider the number of times this "before and after" scenario has repeated itself in the San Juans. (Courtesy of Martin A. Wenger)

Rio Grande Southern derailed

It was the mountains' way of telling the Rio Grande Southern that it did not belong there. Constantly plagued by snow and rock slides, derailments cut deep into the railroad's profits. Washed out bridges, faulty equipment, poor track and grade maintenance — all contributed to the unusually high number of derailments. Combined with the drastic economic downturn, the Rio Grande Southern took a desperate step that has intrigued railroad fans ever since. They created the "Galloping Goose." (Courtesy of P. David Smith)

The Galloping Goose

In an attempt to save their dying railroad, the Rio Grande Southern concocted a strange hybrid, the Galloping Goose, to take the place of expensive passenger trains. "RGS motor No. 2 was the first RGS railbus to be called a 'Galloping Goose.' She was put in service on August 12, 1931, having utilized a Buick six-cylinder motor for motive power" (Collman and McCoy, 1990). She also sported flanged wheels adopted to a three-foot narrow gauge rail. The next Goose was contrived from an old Pierce-Arrow automobile body and engine. Eventually, the Rio Grande Southern built six such contraptions. The half dozen Galloping Geese soon earned more money carrying tourists than mail and parcels.

In this view Galloping Goose No. 3 crosses a newly repaired bridge near Placerville soon after a flood piled debris on both sides of the bridge. No. 3 "was commissioned on December 2, 1931, and was built from a Pierce-Arrow sedan, Model 33. The vehicle had a six-cylinder engine and weighed-in at 14,800 pounds" (Collman and McCoy, 1990). (Postcard: Courtesy of P. David Smith)

The "Galloping Goose" Line

At first the Galloping Geese followed freight trains during winter storms, "to make sure that snowslides or drifts would not stop them dead out along the line" (Collman and McCoy, 1990). During the rest of the year the Geese were on their own.

Soon the Rio Grande Southern started to cater seriously to tourists. Although the tourist trade was not substantial enough to save the railroad, it provided delighted passengers with memorable journeys though scenic locales like Keystone Hill, Ophir Loop, and Trout Lake (above) near Lizard Head Pass.

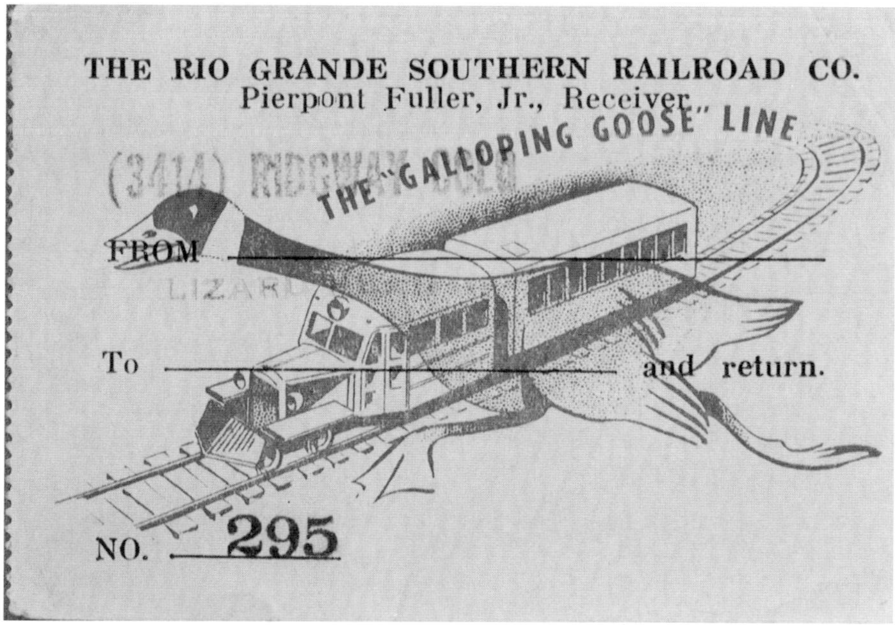
THE RIO GRANDE SOUTHERN RAILROAD CO.
Pierpont Fuller, Jr., Receiver.
THE "GALLOPING GOOSE" LINE
FROM
To
and return.
NO. 295

Passengers riding the Galloping Geese took home appropriately illustrated ticket stubs (right). In 1949 the last Goose expired, ending a unique chapter in railroading history. (Courtesy of Martin A. Wenger) (Author's photo: Courtesy of M. Scott Strain)

Vanadium

Located between Placerville and Telluride along the San Miguel River, the old Vanadium Mine (shown here from a bird's eye view) received a big boost during World War II. Long ignored uranium oxide, a byproduct of vanadium, was discovered to be a key ingredient for the development of America's atomic bomb. "During World War II, Prof. Albert Einstein told President Roosevelt that uranium oxide, a byproduct of vanadium that had been tossed away and ignored for years, had a certain value. Suddenly the lines of the old Southern were filled with a highly valuable deposit guarded by federal agents with machine guns" (Fetter and Fetter, 1979). (Postcard: Courtesy of P. David Smith)

Hardly a trace remains

Except for a few crumbling stone walls, nothing remains of Vanadium or its mine. Not even a sign post marks the spot where they mined the substance that helped unleash the destructive force in two blinding flashes in Nagasaki and Hiroshima and changed the way humans looked at themselves forever. Yet this peculiar Dutch-theme postcard, and an original cancellation stamp from the tiny town, survive. (Author's photos: Courtesy of Bill Ellicott) (Postcard: Courtesy of Joann and Wes Leech)

CHAPTER FIVE: HARD TIMES, BUT GOOD TIMES (1920s-1940s)

In the Vanadium Mine

Two miners blend in with the cribbing and a man sits on a pile of rubble under a menacing overhang in a large stope. Nearly 400 men once worked these large stopes in the Vanadium Mine. Originally called Newmire, between 1898 and 1922 it carried the Primos Chemical Company name. (Telluride Historical Museum)

Parades that impress

An International pickup truck lives up to its name. Bedecked with flags from the United Kingdom, Finland, American Revolutionary War, and the United States, it motors slowly along the parade route. A mounted elk's head tops off its decorations.

Snake-handling Indians dressed in Pow Wow regalia grab the attention of the Fourth of July crowd lining Colorado Avenue. Behind these dancers other members of the group rhythmically beat drums on top of a specially rigged commercial van. (Photos: Telluride Historical Museum)

CHAPTER FIVE: HARD TIMES, BUT GOOD TIMES (1920S-1940S)

The Golden Rule Store

During the 1920s co-owners Irene Wichmann (above, left) and Oscar Wunderlich (second from left) operated the Golden Rule Dry Goods Store out of the old National Club saloon. Later, their store occupied the historic Bank of Telluride building. In the 1940s (below) a fire claimed Sweeny's Barbershop and Beauty Salon next door to the Golden Rule Store. (Photos courtesy of Bill Mahoney)

A railroad no more

The boom began in 1891 with the coming of the Rio Grande Southern Railroad. Sixty years later there were only a few hundred townspeople left to mourn its demise. After a series of disputes with the managers of various Telluride mines, dwindling numbers of tourists, and a debt of $9,000,000 (close to the amount Otto Mears had to raise to get the line running), it folded on September 20, 1951. No longer would people snap photographs of their departing families on the steps of the Telluride depot (above). And no longer would the Rio Grande Southern's whistle echo throughout the San Miguel Valley. Although the boom had long since passed, the collapse of the Rio Grande Southern solidified the economic disaster that enveloped Telluride. (American Heritage Center, University of Wyoming)

Rocky Mountain Railroad Club excursions

During the last years of the Rio Grande Southern's existence, the Rocky Mountain Railroad Club, sensing each time that it might be their last chance, arranged to take excursions on the famous line. Their outing in September 1951 was, in fact, the last passenger run. On this historic trip Rio Grande Southern locomotive No. 74 (above) hauled six carloads of appreciative club members. An earlier rare photograph shows locomotive No. 74 (right) in a roundhouse, thought to be in Ridgway. The locomotive was purchased only three years before the little narrow gauge went bankrupt. Engine No. 74 is now on display in a park in Boulder, Colorado. (O. Perry photo: Denver Public Library, Western History Department) (Courtesy of P. David Smith)

High trestle above Ophir

In the late 1940s an excursion train chugs across a high trestle, part of the world-famous Ophir Loop. On the gravel road below, now Highway 145, cars and trucks covered the same distance more quickly, easily, and cheaply. That too, contributed to the Rio Grande Southern's demise. (R. Richardson photo: Denver Public Library, Western History Department)

A good economic run

In forlorn Telluride the Rio Grande Southern tracks are torn up, the water tank stands empty, and not a soul is in sight. In 1942, Telluride Mines Incorporated purchased the Tomboy and the adjoining mines, but steadily declining zinc and lead prices forced its closure in 1953 — another devastating blow to the town. Then the Idarado Mining Company of New York bought most of the famous old Telluride mines, connecting them with over 350 miles of tunnels. After removing millions of dollars in ore, it ceased operations in 1978.

Telluride had a good economic run. And little did any of its townspeople know another, even bigger, economic run would soon come. Some say that it is best not to debate the merits of such boom-and-bust cycles. Better to enjoy the booms while they last. (R. Richardson photo: Denver Public Library, Western History Department)

CHAPTER FIVE: HARD TIMES, BUT GOOD TIMES (1920s-1940s)

BIBLIOGRAPHY

H
I
S
T
O
R
I
C

T
E
L
L
U
R
I
D
E

I
N

R
A
R
E

P
H
O
T
O
G
R
A
P
H
S

Adams, E. B. (date unknown). *Gio Oberto of Telluride, Colorado*. Grand Junction, Colorado: Private printing. (Courtesy of Dr. Jim Parker).

Backus, H. F. (1969). *Tomboy Bride*. Boulder, Colorado: Pruett Publishing Company.

Bailey, S. A. (1933). *L. L. Nunn, a Memoir*. Ithaca, New York: Cayuga Press.

Belsey Jr., G. W. (1962). "When to Telluride, to Helluride!" Unpublished manuscript. (Courtesy of Alta Cassietto).

Brown, R. L. (1963: 1983 reprint). *Jeep Trails to Colorado Ghost Towns*. Caldwell, Idaho: Caxton Printers, Ltd.

Brown, R. L. (1968). *An Empire of Silver*. Caldwell, Idaho: Caxton Printers, Ltd.

Buys, C. J. (1986). "Accounts of the Battle at Milk Creek: Implications for Historical Accuracy." *Essays and Monographs in Colorado History*, Number 4, 59 - 80.

Buys, C. J. (1986). "Power in the Mountains: Lucien Nunn Catapults the San Juans into the Age of Electricity." *Colorado Heritage*, Volume 4, 25 - 37.

Buys, C. J. (1993). "Fort Crawford: A Symbol of Transition." *Journal of the Western Slope*, Volume 8 (2), 1 - 29.

Buys, C. J. (1997). *Historic Leadville in Rare Photographs and Drawings*. Ouray, Colorado: Western Reflections Publishing.

Buys, C. J. (1997: summer issue). "Of Frozen Fire Hydrants and 'Drunkin Sons of a Bitches', Early Leadville's Volunteer Firemen." *Colorado Heritage*, 2 - 15.

Collman, R., and McCoy, D. A. (1990). *The R.G.S. [Rio Grande Southern] Story: Volume I — "Over the Bridges — Ridgway to Telluride"*. Denver, Colorado: Sundance Publications, Ltd.

Collman, R., and McCoy, D. A. (1991). *The R.G.S. [Rio Grande Southern] Story: Volume II — "Telluride, Pandora, and the Mines Above"*. Denver, Colorado: Sundance Publications, Ltd.

Collman, R., McCoy, D. A., and Graves, W. A. (1993). *The R.G.S. [Rio Grande Southern] Story: Volume III — Over the Bridges . . . Vance Junction to Ophir*. Denver, Colorado: Sundance Publications, Ltd.

Collman, R., McCoy, D. A., and Graves, W. A. (1994). *The R.G.S. [Rio Grande Southern] Story: Volume IV — Over the Bridges . . . Ophir Loop to Rico*. Denver, Colorado: Sundance Publications, Ltd.

Crofutt, G. A. (1885: 1981 reprint). *Grip-Sack Guide of Colorado, 1885*. Boulder, Colorado: Johnson Publishing Company.

Crum, J. M. (1954: 1961 reprint). *The Rio Grande Southern Railroad*. Durango, Colorado: San Juan History (Hamilton Press).

Dorman, R. L. (1994). *The Rio Grande Southern II, An Ultimate Pictorial Study*. RD Publications: Santa Fe, New Mexico.

Fetter, R. L., and Fetter, S. (1979: 1990 reprint). *Telluride: "From Pick to Powder."* Caldwell, Idaho: Caxton Printers.

Gregory, M., and Smith, P. D. (1984). *Mountain Mysteries: The Ouray Odyssey*. Ouray, Colorado: Wayfinder Press.

Gressley, G. M. (ed.) (1968). *Bostonians and Bullion: The Journal of Robert Livermore, 1892 - 1915*. Lincoln, Nebraska: University of Nebraska Press.

Lavender, D. (1943: 1977 reprint). *One Man's West*. Lincoln, Nebraska: University of Nebraska Press.

Lavender, D. (1964). *A Rocky Mountain Fantasy, Telluride, Colorado*. Telluride, Colorado: San Miguel County Historical Society.

Lavender, D. (with photography by G. H. H. Huey). (1987). *The Telluride Story*. Ridgway, Colorado: Wayfinder Press.

Maness, P., and Jacobs, L. (date unknown). *"The Loop."* Grand Junction, Colorado: Private printing.

McCoy, D. A., Collman, R., and Graves, W. A. (1996). *The R.G.S. [Rio Grande Southern] Story: Volume V — Rico and the Mines*. Denver, Colorado: Sundance Publications, Ltd.

McDougald, C. (1997). "Poles and the Men Who Love Them." *Crown Jewels of The Wire*, Volume 29 (1), 15 - 32.

Ordinances of the City of Telluride, 1917. (1917). Telluride, Colorado: San Miguel Examiner (City Council of Telluride).

"Pioneers of the San Juan Country, Vol. I." (1942). By the Sarah Platt Decker Chapter of the D.A.R. of Durango, Colorado. Colorado Springs: The Out West Printing and Stationery Company. (Courtesy of Bill Ellicot)

"St. Patrick's Church, Sixtieth Anniversary, 1896 - 1956, Telluride, Colorado." (1956). Montrose, Colorado: Montrose Daily Press. (Courtesy of Bill Ellicott)

Tallman, R. (1907). Unpublished correspondence. (Courtesy of Dr. James Parker).

Telluride and San Miguel County, Colorado. (1894). Denver, Colorado: The Publishers Press Room Company (Telluride Board of Trade).

Tonge, T. (1913). *All About Colorado*. Denver, Colorado: Smith-Brooks Printing Co.

Wagner, Bessie. (date unknown). "A Few Notes about Pioneer Mining in the Telluride, Colorado, Area." Unpublished manuscript. (Courtesy of Bill Mahoney).

Weber, R. (1974). *A Quick History of Telluride*. Colorado Springs, Colorado: Little London Press.

Wenger, M. G. (1978: 1989 reprint). *Recollections of Telluride Colorado: 1895 - 1920*. Durango, Colorado: Private printing.

Western Colorado Power Collection (Boxes 1 - 5) held by the Center of Southwest Studies, Fort Lewis College, Durango, Colorado.

Wichmann, I. (date unknown). "History of Telluride." Unpublished manuscript. (Courtesy of Alta Cassietto).

Wolle, M. S. (1949). *Stampede to Timberline*. Boulder, Colorado: Private printing.

Wood, F., and Wood, D. (1977). *"I Hauled These Mountains in Here."* Caldwell, Idaho: Caxton Printers, Ltd.

Wright, A. (1974). "Mining town doctor." *Daily Sentinel*, May 26. Grand Junction, Colorado.

HISTORIC TELLURIDE IN RARE PHOTOGRAPHS